TRAINING YOUR

RABBIT

Patricia Bartlett

Second Edition

BARRON'S

Acknowledgments

I want to express my appreciation to Round Da Bend Rabbitry owned by Tanya & Andy Zimmerman, Clintonville WI; Aase Bjerner; Senoria Clarke; Sarah Breaupre; W. Tullett of West Yorkshire; Arthur Bijker; Maria Cramer of Willowbrook Rabbitry; Jason C. K. Chan; Marna Kazmaier of RabbitAgility.com; Gary Van Fleet; Dave Smith; Kathy Finelli and Betsy Day of Gainesville (FL) Rabbit Rescue; Greg Fleming, DVM; Patty Nemeth; Leslie Seddon of Sunrise Creek Farm; Scott Wenzel of South Mountain Rabbitry; Dawn Nelsey of A Basket of Blessings Rabbitry; Sophie Louis, Jo Hinde, RVN; Kate Mackinnon, Rosemary and Amanda Greening of the Canadian Hopping Club; and all those individuals who have worked for rabbit rescue, agility, and hopping.

As always, I thank Dick Bartlett for his support and help whenever I asked, and my editor, Anthony Regolino, who somehow keeps on top of changes in the publishing field.

About the Author

Patricia Bartlett writes pet care books, reptile and amphibian field guides, and books on Florida history and hobbies.

Photo Credits

Joan Balzarini: 71, 82; Patricia Bartlett: 2, 4 (bottom), 6, 8 (bottom), 9 (bottom), 18, 21, 28, 29 (top), 30, 31 (top and bottom), 33, 38 (bottom), 41, 45, 46 (top), 48 (bottom), 73, 78, 81 (bottom); R. D. Bartlett: 80; Sarah Beaupre: 20; Norvia Behling: 22 (bottom), 63 (top); Arthur Bijker: 8 (top); Nora Clarke: 5, 9 (top), 48 (top), 50 (bottom); Maria Cramer: 3 (top and bottom), 4 (bottom); G. J. Fleming: 81; Amanda Greening: 32, 59, 65, 69; Daniel Johnson/Paulette Johnson: 7, 10, 11 (top and bottom), 12, 13, 14, 15, 16, 17, 22 (top), 24, 25 (top), 29 (bottom), 34 (top and bottom), 36 (top and bottom), 38 (top), 39, 40, 42, 43, 46 (bottom), 50 (top), 51, 54, 55, 57 (top and bottom), 58 (top), 62, 72, 75, 87, 88, 90, 91; Sophie Louis: 1, 25 (bottom), 44, 58 (bottom); Dave Smith: 61, 64, 66 (bottom), 68; W. Tullett: 66 (top); Gary Van Fleet: 35, 37, 70.

Cover Photos

Daniel Johnson/Paulette Johnson: inside back cover; Shutterstock: front cover, back cover, inside front cover.

All inquiries should be addressed to:
Barron's Educational Series, Inc.
250 Wireless Boulevard
Hauppauge, New York 11788
www.barronseduc.com

ISBN: 978-1-4380-0034-3

Library of Congress Control Number: 2012003688

Library of Congress Cataloging-in-Publication Data
Bartlett, Patricia Pope, 1949–
  Training your pet rabbit / Patricia Bartlett. — 2nd ed.
    p. cm.
  Includes bibliographical references and index.
  ISBN 978-1-4380-0034-3
  1. Rabbits. 2. Rabbits—Training. I. Title.
  SF453.B37 2012
  636.932'2—dc23   2012003688

Printed in China
987654321

Important Note
While handling rabbits, you may occasionally receive bites or scratches. If your skin is broken, contact your physician immediately.

Rabbits may transmit certain infections to humans. Always wash your hands carefully after handling your specimens. And always supervise children who wish to observe or handle your rabbits.

Contents

Chapter One
Where It All Began

That wide-eyed little rabbit you've been thinking about training is a descendant of the European wild rabbit, *Oryctolagus cuniculus*. But the wild rabbit didn't exactly jump into domestic life, first as a food source and then as a pet. There were some unavoidable delays first, starting with very cold weather.

The last Ice Age—the one that ended about 11,000 years ago—pushed this rabbit from its wide distribution in Europe southward, onto the Iberian Peninsula, and into what is now France. Its reintroduction into Europe had to wait for several thousand years and for human intervention.

The human intervention part began with the Phoenicians, traders extraordinaire (dealers in ivory, foods, and other trade goods from what is now Lebanon, Israel, and Syria). They came to the Iberian Peninsula about 1100 B.C. in search of raw materials for the Middle Eastern market. As the Phoenicians progressed further into their exploration across the Iberian Peninsula, they were particularly pleased to find two very marketable items. The first was large silver deposits. The second was a species of murex. This particular kind of murex, found off the coast, secreted a purple dye used for the clothing of royalty. Both were valuable as trade items and essentially free for the taking.

The Phoenicians settled into Spain and founded colonies, one of

A fuzzy lop leaps up to play with soap bubbles.

The standard domestic rabbit still bears the scientific name of the European rabbit.

which was Gafir (now Cadiz) on the Atlantic coast northwest of Gibraltar. Gafir became a major export post, its location meshing nicely with northern ports and those along the southern and eastern borders of the Mediterranean, northern Africa, and Morocco.

The Phoenicians were quick to see the practical side of rabbits, and they utilized them as a free and readily available source of meat and fur. Rabbits were easy to cage, feed, and transport. Their dried or salted meat was a ready trade item.

But nothing lasts forever, and that's particularly true of human dynasties. The Phoenician trading network collapsed near the end of the sixth century B.C., and the nearby Carthaginians, living in what is today's Tunis, moved into southern Spain.

The Punic War displaced the Carthaginians in favor of the Romans (there's a lot more to Spain's history than this, but since we're focusing on rabbits, we'll keep the history part short).

The Romans managed to hang onto Iberia from about 200 B.C. to 600 A.D. During this time, as part of their quest to expand the Roman Empire, they headed northward to England. It took them two tries, but the second effort in 43 A.D. paid off. Romans occupied England until about 400 A.D. Along with massive public works like bridges and roads, the Romans left behind them evidence of their daily lives, and that evidence includes rabbit remains. A Roman rubbish pit excavated near Lynford, Norfolk, yielded early Roman pottery, Iron Age items dating back to Roman occupation and the butchered remains of a European rabbit. This evidence puts rabbits into England earlier than the Normandy invasion (1066 A.D., in case you've forgotten), which previously was thought to be the time rabbits were brought to England.

The Romans took rabbits to northern Africa as well. DNA analysis indicates the European rabbit was introduced to Tunisia, a country at northernmost mid-Africa, south of the tip of Italy's boot, about 2000 years ago. The oldest bones come from late Roman layers, third to fourth century A.D.

By the Middle Ages captive rabbits were present throughout Europe. Rabbit warrens were con-

Lopapalooza: From the left: French Lop, an English Lop, a Mini Lop, an American Fuzzy Lop, and a Holland Lop. They are arranged by size, largest to smallest.

structed in southern France during the tenth century and for a while could only be owned by nobles. Bur escapees were inevitable, and "wild" European rabbits became established. This brought them into literal reach of anyone clever enough to set a trap or pull young rabbits out of a warren. By the sixteenth century, domestic rabbit keeping as we know it began.

With the development of domestic rabbit breeding, different traits began to appear; they were noted, and line breeding began for different traits. An early heavy weight was a primary objective, although rabbits with different colors of fur were also prized. In 1631, a booklet on rabbit breeding by a writer named Gervaise Marrkham advised rabbit breeders to breed from the largest rabbits (called "conies"). Marrkham heralded the meat attri-

butes of a rabbit that sounds very much like today's heavy-bodied meat breed, the Champagne D'Argent. Marrkham's description was of a "silvered" rabbit with rich fur, and "the best specimens hath the equallest mixture of blacke

The Champagne d'Argent, one of the earliest breeds, turns from black to gray as it matures.

Doug Cramer holds Camille, a championship French Lop.

development of individual domestic rabbit breeds prior to the late 1800s is a bit tricky. One can find written descriptions of rabbits, and even earlier artwork that seems to describe a particular breed. For instance, English lops are gorgeous large meat rabbits with long basset hound-like ears. Because of their size and their ears, they are one of the earliest of the recognizable breeds. What sounds like a lop-eared rabbit is cited in an 1821 pamphlet. The pamphlet mentions rabbits being kept as pets, unusual at that time because rabbits were a meat source. These pet rabbits were spotted, black and tortoise colored with fine long ears "which occasion their falling about the head, in manner different from the common rabbit."

and white haire together, yet the blacke rather shadowing the white; the furre should be thicke, deepe, smooth, and shining," qualities the Champagne D'Argent breeders feel could be their rabbit type.

With no written breeding records, trying to track down the actual

By the middle 1800s, breeds such as the Champagne D'Argent, the lop, and the Flemish Giant had appeared, followed by the Beveren and the Britannia Petite.

In the late 1800s one meat breed took off in popularity, a bit like the tulip bulb craze in the early 1600s in Holland, but not quite that expensive. The object is this case was a big rabbit called the Belgian Hare. Originally from the Flanders area of east Europe, their name acknowledged the area of their origin and their resemblance to the English hare. Belgian Hares were exported first to England (1870s) and then to the United States (1880s), both times with considerable fanfare and publicity.

Selective breeding has produced the velvety Rex. Their fur lacks the coarser guard hair.

Flemish Giants are 15–18 pounds at adulthood.

This prolific rabbit was heralded as an easy-to-raise, delicious meat source, and direct competitor to poultry. G. L. M. Arkinson, author of several glowing pamphlets of the advantages of raising the Belgian Hare, wrote the Belgian Hare had "proven to be the rich man's fancy and the poor man's friend." Hotel restaurants picked up the banner and created dishes featuring Belgian Hare at Christmas.

Belgians hit it big in the United States, and by 1900 they were particularly popular in California. Bucks (males) sold for as much as $2500 (and in those days, $2500 was a huge amount of money). Breeding colonies were set up and breeders and wanna-be breeders knew prosperity was just around the corner.

The dream was a lot brighter than the truth. Despite their size, the light-boned Belgian Hare didn't carry a lot of meat. The Belgian Hare was a big eater—they were big rabbits—but they didn't "weigh out" well. That made the return on investment a bit lower than what was hoped for.

And not everyone was crazy about bringing the Belgian to the United States as a food source. A 1900 report to the Maine Commissioners of Inland Game and Fish cautioned that state about importing the Belgian Hare, pointing out how easy it would be for the Belgian Hare to become established in Maine due to its reproduction rate and modest food and housing needs. The report suggested the Commissioners of Inland Fisheries and Game regulate the potential introduction of any nonnative bird or animal. (Worries about invasive species were a concern even then.)

By 1915, other rabbit breeds that were less flighty and bulkier were

Smaller rabbit breeds are popular as pets. Sterling, a Dwarf Netherlands, noses Sassafras, a Mini-Lop.

competing with the Belgian for a spot on the American dinner plate, and ads in the *Poultry Tribune* were offering Belgians at reduced prices. By the start of World War I, the Belgian Hare had been replaced by other rabbit breeds as a select meat producer. Today there are only three Belgian Hare breeders listed in the America Rabbit Breeders Association directory (by way of comparison, more than forty New Zealand White breeders are listed).

But the fervent Belgian Hare fanciers did leave a legacy behind that has benefited all rabbit fanciers, whether for meat or companionship. They founded the American Belgian Hare Association Fanciers Club, which was succeeded by the National Belgian Hare Club of America in 1897. Just twelve years later, the American Pet Stock Association (APSA) was founded ("pet stock" is like "livestock," meaning pets supplied as stock for stores and meat producers). The APSA evolved into the American Rab-

bit Breeders Association (ARBA), a group now dedicated to the domestic rabbit and cavy (guinea pig) fancy in the United States.

The ARBA is the go-to group that recognizes some fifty rabbit breeds (this includes five of the new breeds recognized at the 2011 convention, the Silver Martin Mini Rex, the Blue Rhinelander, the Blue Tortoiseshell Netherlands Dwarf, and the Chinchilla Dutch). England recognizes about eighty breeds. Breeds are determined by body type/shape, ear shape/position, color/pattern, and alertness/nervousness.

In case you're thinking about developing a new breed of rabbit, it takes about ten years to get recognized by the ARBA; they don't grant breed status lightly. During the selective breeding process that results in a new breed of rabbits such as the Lionhead, other characteristics are selectively being bred out, those being fear of humans, nipping, and failure to thrive under captive conditions.

Today's ARBA is primarily a meat rabbit producers' and cavy owners' association, promoting, developing, and improving the domestic rabbit and cavy. Pet and house rabbit owners are very much a part of the group. ARBA welcomes house rabbit owners' memberships, but if it bothers you to see the latest prices per pound of rabbit meat in each issue of their monthly magazine, this may not be the organization for you.

Chapter Two
Selecting and Bonding with Your Rabbit

How do you know which bunny breed is the best as a pet? If you are interested in buying a specific kind of rabbit, like a Havana or a Lionhead, the individuals who breed and show rabbits and the commercial rabbit dealers would be happy to talk and deal with you. Pet stores that sell rabbits would be pleased to see you walk in the door (although their selection as far as specific rabbit breeds might be very limited). But if you're interested in "just a rabbit," you have several search methods.

You can check your local classified ads, Craigslist, or Petfinder.com for rabbits. Be aware that many of these rabbits are available because the owner bought/acquired the rabbit and discovered that the rabbit didn't want to sit in the owner's lap, or stayed in the back of its cage rather than frisking around when the new owner approached. You know shyness is a totally natural rabbit behavior, but people sometimes acquire pets without any idea of what to expect.

Keep in mind that the rabbits on Craigslist or in classified ads or

listed on note cards stuck up at the local feed store in all likelihood have not been neutered or spayed, so that a "free to a good home" rabbit won't exactly be free. It will need to be neutered or spayed. Neutering or spaying will cost a minimum of $100, unless your local humane society has low-cost vouchers you can buy. If the rabbit is female, like that stray female cat your neighbors took in last month, she may be pregnant. (Most new rabbit owners have no idea how readily a female rabbit can become pregnant. Rabbits are very efficient. The female ovulates upon being

If supervised, a house rabbit, like this Holland Lop, can spend hours out of his cage.

Gucci the lionhead sits up and waits to be petted.

bred by a male. One "exposure" and she's pregnant. Rabbit people generally call these "oopsie" litters.)

An even better source would be your local animal shelter or rabbit rescue group. Rabbits at animal shelters generally stay there a limited time before they are put to sleep, and rescue groups try to "pull" these rabbits and put them into their own foster rabbit system before their time runs out at the shelter. But the rescue groups run out of space as well.

If you find a rabbit you like at a shelter, you'll need to fill out a minimal amount of paperwork, assuring them that you'll take good care of the rabbit and promising not to turn it loose. You'll have to pay a fee, usually between $10 and $45. A rabbit from an animal shelter probably will need to be spayed or neutered, but there are exceptions. One of the shelters in Florida neuters and microchips all the male rabbits that came into their shelter, but this sort of service is unusual. Humane societies often sell low-cost spay or neuter certificates you can use at your local veterinarian to pay for the surgery (yes, even for rabbits!), and that may save you perhaps half of what the surgery would cost otherwise.

Your compensation for this extra expense is that you've gained a furry friend AND saved a rabbit's life.

Rabbits from a rabbit rescue group are more expensive, from $50 to $145, because the rabbit

Ninety percent of marketing is getting the customer to pick up the item—in this case, a very pettable Rex rabbit.

will already be spayed or neutered. One of these rabbits may still be a deal because you don't have to go out and get the certificate from your humane society and you don't have to deal with finding a veterinarian. Even if your rabbit is spayed or neutered, you should find a rabbit-knowledgeable veterinarian, preferably prior to adopting your new companion.

Another advantage to a rescue rabbit is that the volunteers there work with the rabbits in their care, and they know a little bit about the individual rabbits. The rabbit foster parent can tell you if a particular rabbit is good with dogs and cats, if it is OK with children, or even more exactly, if the rabbit is good with the litter box. You can get a report on any rabbit you're thinking of adopting.

Rabbit rescue groups are also fussy about the people they allow to adopt rabbits. Rabbits that come into rescue have already been discarded once, and rescue groups screen potential adopters to help make sure it doesn't happen again. They'll want to know if there are any other pets in the home, or if there are any children (kids younger than 7 or 8 are too young to understand why they ought not to pick up a rabbit, or that a rabbit needs a place to get to where he can't be bothered by humans). Children don't mean to be rough with rabbits, but small rabbits have small bones. It's often best to place larger rabbits—rabbits that are just

Rabbits can be steadfast friends with other animals.

On a chilly day, your rabbit may enjoy snuggling in a towel.

9

Indoor caging is simple to set up using dog kennel panels.

too big to be picked up by kids—in homes with children.

The rabbit rescue group will also generally make a home visit to see where you plan on placing your rabbit. Is the cage large enough? What about out of cage time? Rabbit rescue groups generally won't adopt-out a rabbit to a home with an outside hutch; rescue groups place house rabbits, not outdoors rabbits.

Creating a bond with your rabbit

You need to establish a relationship with your rabbit before you can train him, and this means you have to spend time with him, daily. You need to hang out together, so to speak, so he knows you a bit and you know him, and so the two of you can learn to trust each other. You are, of course, a human, a member of a group with some history of being unable to fulfill promises. You need to hold up your end of the bargain and work to bond with your rabbit.

Plan to spend 15 to 30 minutes at a time with your rabbit, in his pen or in a room in your house. Your goal is to get your rabbit to feel safe when he is playing or sitting near you, and for him to enjoy eating treats and being petted and talked to. You want your rabbit to see you as nonthreatening, first, and then as a source of petting.

You can do this by joining him in his pen, and letting him come up to you when he feels like it. You don't have to do much; just sit on the floor in his pen with him. Talk to him. Bring a book and read. Reward your rabbit for hopping toward you with a leaf of romaine lettuce or a small carrot piece. Hold the food and let him take it from your fingers.

Spend part of the time you're waiting by watching your rabbit. My new New Zealand white sniffed in the direction of the papaya treat I held in my hand, and firmly turned her back on me. She acted so much like a class-conscious human being I found myself saying "Hey, wait a minute," stopping of course before I actually uttered a word. A day later she hopped over to me and ate the mini carrot stick while I held it.

Your rabbit may act as if you aren't even there. He may decide it's time to wash his face and paws, sitting up on his haunches and licking his paws and rubbing them over his face and ears. He may sit back in his cage and watch you. Wiggle the food piece a bit and talk to him. Some rabbit keepers try to reassure their rabbits with like behaviors. They groom themselves, running their hands over their face and hair. This seems to reassure some bunnies that the human in front of them is not a threat.

It takes a bit of patience to outwait a rabbit. Just practice sitting there. For the first few visits, you

Handling your rabbit during training includes careful "hand-overs" from one person to another.

want your rabbit to accept your food treat and your presence. Yes, this is bribery, but it works.

Wear blue jeans or other heavy pants to protect your legs and to give your bunny-in-training secure footing.

As your rabbit approaches you more consistently, talk to him. You can work toward petting him (start with just a light petting touch on the forehead, going in the direction of the fur) when he's near you. When he crouches down and closes his eye as you tickle him around his ears, you're making progress.

If your rabbit is in a cage, you can begin the bonding process by putting the cage where you will see it, and the bunny will see you. The living room or room adjacent to the kitchen is a good idea; just make sure your rabbit isn't stuck in a cage with no chance of human interaction. If you can elevate the cage so your rabbit is easier to talk to, so much the better. Your rabbit has little to do in a cage by himself. You need to be his entertainment and his friend.

Put your rabbit down safely by cradling him in your hands and then do a gentle "turn" so his feet are on the ground as you release him.

In addition to sitting next to the cage and talking to your new pet several times a day, open the door and let him come to the opening and peer out. It may take 15 minutes the first few times, but he will come to the open door. Reward him when he comes to the door with a treat—but he has to come to the door first.

Once your bunny hops to the door of his cage at your approach, you can begin handling him. Simply open the cage and pick him up, using one hand under his rib cage and the other under his rump, so even if he kicks, he won't make contact with you. Be ready to deal with the adjustment in his balance if he kicks; don't let him kick himself out of your hands. For a secure hold, you can turn him so his face is tucked into the bend of your elbow. Support his body with that same forearm and hand; your hand curls around his rump to hold him securely against your body. You need to learn to hold your rabbit so he won't kick and injure you or himself. (Rabbits can kick so hard they can actually break those fine bones, and those claws can *hurt*.)

Sit down in a chair and move the rabbit so he is sitting beside you or he is on your lap looking toward you. Long pants or a towel will protect your legs should he kick or try to launch himself off your lap.

Hold your rabbit in place with your hands and talk to him. Stroke him a bit on his head, gently, and tickle the part between his eyes and

A house rabbit has found a clever hiding spot so he can watch you unobserved.

ears. As you did in sitting in his pen or next to his cage, you want to have your rabbit become accustomed to the sound of your voice, to your touch, and to the sensation of being held and to associate all contact with you as pleasant and possibly treat-connected.

Hold him for a few minutes and then return him to his cage, being careful as you place him inside that he doesn't kick his way out of your grasp. Place the rabbit into the cage hind-end first to prevent the rabbit's trying to jump into the cage and injuring itself. Reward him through the cage bars with a bit of a treat in his cage as you end the session. You want to make any contact with you a positive event.

Your rabbit may take a while to respond to you. Rabbits that have been discarded may have been subjected to loud voices and less than gentle handling. Their former owner found he or she really didn't have time for a pet rabbit, or found that a rabbit is not like a dog or a cat. Your rabbit may not have been handled very much before it was placed into rescue, so he's not going to be enthused about your picking him up and holding him; he just doesn't know what it means. Be patient with your rabbit and with yourself. You will be amazed at the quality of affection that your bunny can develop toward you, and how much he will enjoy being trained when affection is the only reward.

they are lagomorphs, having two sets of gnawing teeth in the upper jaw. (Rats and other rodents have one set of gnawing teeth in the upper jaw.) They evolved on a dried grass diet, and they have turned that capability to an enormous environmental advantage. They can live well where other herbivores can't make the grade. They can do this because food passes through their gut twice, so the maximum nutritional value can be wrested from every bit. Most people don't know this, so if you share this knowledge with others, be prepared to hear comments such as "Gross" or "Yuck."

Since you'd like your rabbit to live its full life of 8 to 10 years, providing the correct diet is important. The good news is that this is remarkably easy to do. Provide plenty of water and unlimited hay, fresh greens daily, and limit the amount of rabbit pellets you feed.

Water is important because rabbits are especially vulnerable to dehydration. They must never be without a source of clean water.

Diet and selecting treats

A rabbit's life span is in many ways directly related to its diet. Rabbits are herbivores, and they are essentially grazing herbivores. Although you may have thought in the past that rabbits are rodents,

Table 1
Comparative content by percentages

	Grass hay	Timothy	Alfalfa	Wheat straw
Protein	14	8	16	3
Fiber	31	30	28	35
Calcium	0.4	0.5	1.5	0.2

For them, unlimited access to water and food is critical to their health. A rabbit that does not eat for more than 24 hours needs to be seen by a veterinarian immediately! Use a heavy ceramic water bowl, or one of the rabbit watering bottles with a metal spout that hangs on the outside of the cage.

Hay provides the long fiber that rabbits need for gut mobility and helps to maintain good dental health. Hay as a main diet item avoids a lot of diet-related problems.

Pellets belong in a varied diet, but they should not be offered as the only dietary choice.

"What's this about rabbit pellets?" you may ask, "Rabbit pellets have been around for a long time, and zillions of rabbits are fed nothing else and do just fine. I can buy the pellets in my grocery store, for goodness' sakes."

You're right about those zillions of rabbits, but the majority of

---

Table 2
Homegrown treats

If you've got a garden area, or a sunny windowsill, you can grow your own treats for your rabbit. Offer these in addition to the usual daily greens. Here are some she'll enjoy (and yes, you can have some, too).

- Basil
- Beet greens
- Borage
- Broccoli
- Brussels sprouts
- Carrots and carrot tops
- Turnips/rutabagas
- Catnip and catmint
- Cauliflower
- Cilantro
- Comfrey
- Dandelion
- Kale
- Lemon Grass
- Lovage
- Mints (orange mint, spearmint, pennyroyal, pineapple mint, apple mint, golden apple mint)
- Nasturtium
- Oregano
- Parsley
- Parsnip
- Raspberry leaves
- Squash

Your house rabbit will soon learn the rustle of a plastic produce bag means "treat!"

those rabbits are raised as meat. Rabbits intended for use as food themselves are fed rabbit pellets to make them bulk up quickly. These rabbits are sized-up for about a hundred days, or until they reach the magic weight of 5 pounds, and then they are harvested. The long-term effects of *their* rabbit pellet diet are moot. Your rabbit doesn't need to be a hundred-day wonder.

Rabbit pellets are low in long fiber and don't provide enough work for the rabbit's gut. Rabbits fed a diet that's too low in fiber can develop gastric stasis, a very bad condition in which the diges-

An unsupervised house rabbit will nibble on anything, including books.

tion process comes to a stop. Your first and most obvious indication of a diet that's too low in fiber is chronically soft stools. Provide hay to your rabbit so he has fiber. (Keep an eye on him nonetheless; soft stools aren't a good sign.)

Because dried rabbit pellets are a compressed or condensed food, the calcium levels are higher than they would be for just the grass used to make the pellets. Your pet can end up with calcium-overload problems like kidney stones and bladder stones, especially if for some reason your rabbit's fresh water supply has been limited. One of our rescue rabbits went off his feed about the second day we had him. His alert fosterer realized it was something more than a minor digestive upset and whisked him off to the veterinarian. One X-ray later, we had the diagnosis, a bladder stone, due we think in this case to his pellets-only diet and caging/water that would have been marginal in winter and potentially deadly in summer's heat. But pellet-only diets are not the only reason for urinary tract stones in rabbits. Other dietary items that are high in calcium, like alfalfa, as well as genetic and environmental factors can contribute to stone formation, and rabbits on pellet-free diets can develop stones. Kidney and bladder stones are as uncomfortable for rabbits as they are for humans. Surgery is the answer, and you need to hope the trauma will be well tolerated.

Rabbit pellets have another point against them. They are higher in protein than hay, and higher protein levels in the diet create higher ammonia levels in the urine. (This is true in humans as well, so think twice about a high-protein diet). High ammonia levels in the air not only stink to high heaven but, when coupled with poor ventilation (as in a small room), set your rabbit up for problems with his lungs. Your rabbit could come down with pasteurellosis, a highly infectious disease that often attacks lung tissue weakened by high levels of ammonia. That's one of the reasons you want caging with plenty of ventilation. A cage with plenty of ventilation also clues you into knowing the litter box needs cleaning.

Rabbits respond well to carrots and apples as training rewards.

What to feed

Feed your rabbit mixed grasses such as timothy hay, coastal hay, oat grass, and meadow grass (alfalfa hay is less desirable because of its higher calcium content). You can buy these dried products by-the-bale or by the bag at pet stores and feed stores. The storage area needs to be dry, to prevent the hay from getting moldy, and frankly a bale or half bale may last you a lot longer than is desirable.

Another reason for feeding dried grasses is their laudable abrasive effect on your rabbit's teeth. Grass contains varying amounts of silica, depending on the type of grass.

Rabbits' teeth grow continuously, to deal with the wear inflicted on them by their diet of dried grass. The teeth grow continuously no matter what diet your rabbit is on. Rabbits' incisors grow 3 mm/week, the cheek molars 3 mm a month. If a wild rabbit is removed from the wild and fed a diet exclusively of pellets, he will exhibit elongated cheek teeth within 2 weeks. Baby wild rabbits that are weaned onto pellets develop skull and teeth malformations because their teeth don't get enough wear. Grass is important.

Rabbit pellets contain the vitamins your rabbit needs in the correct proportions. Provide ¼ to ½-cup of pellets per 5 pounds of rabbit weight twice a day. Your

Think "dark green" when shopping for salads for your rabbit.

hay down in the cage and let your rabbit simply snack on it as is. Many rabbit owners just put the hay in one end of the litter box. There are rabbit owners who don't like this placement, pointing out that it is far too likely that the hay will become soiled with urine and feces before it can be consumed. If you still want to keep hay in the kitty box, provide additional clean hay in another part of the cage at the same time. You can provide a little fun/enrichment as you place the hay. Put the hay in chewable baskets, in an empty oatmeal box, or in a clean tin can. (Be certain you use pliers to crimp flat the sharp edges of the can before you use it for hay. Your fingers will tell you if there are any sharp edges left.) You can stuff hay into a paper bag, fold the opening over to close the bag, and put it into the cage. Your rabbit will figure out in short order how to tear into the bag, and may hide cunningly in the undestroyed portion of the bag as he eats.

You can use a suet feeder from your local bird store. Use wire cutters to nip out sections of the sides and top to create openings that are 1–2 inches (3 to 5 cm) across, and then stuff the suet feeder with hay.

I took both ends out of a tin can and stuffed the hay inside. My rabbits enjoyed snacking on the hay and leaping onto the tin can during the small hours of the morning. (Eventually my dogs stopped barking at the sound.) The tin can also made it essentially impossi-

average 7-pound rabbit would get between 3/8 to ¾ cups of pellets a day, in addition to his greens and unlimited hay. I kept a heavy ceramic dish in my rabbits' cage for their pellets. My lop rabbits would empty the dish and scoot it around with their little flat noses as a hint when it was empty.

Rabbit raisers, especially those who raise rabbits for food, know female rabbits (called does) that are nursing litters need large amounts of food. They tend to offer a nursing doe all the pellets she will consume. They only decrease the quantity of pellets just before the young are born or kindled, just after the young are born, and when the young are weaned at 4 to 5 weeks. Decreasing the food supply at these times helps prevent a condition called caked udder, when the milk production is too heavy.

Rabbits should have all the dried hay they want. You can plunk the

ble for my rabbits to urinate on the uneaten portion, something they tended to do when I simply flopped a double handful of hay into the cage.

In addition to the hay, your rabbit needs fresh greens, the high-fiber, deep green kinds your mother always wanted you to eat. Now you can buy greens and assure your mom that they are on your grocery list every week. Every day, provide your rabbit with greens like kale, collard greens, parsley, dandelion greens, chicory, mustard greens, romaine lettuce, basil, endive, and Swiss chard. Provide a packed cupful every night. (The general guidelines are a half cup for every pound of rabbit, but you may find that your rabbits won't consume that much, and I hate to compute the cost of feeding 3½ cups of mixed salad greens to my New Zealand White every night.)

Alternately, just buy three types of greens at a time, and offer all sometime each week. If you haven't tried mustard greens instead of spinach in your own spinach salad, you might find the sharp flavor to your liking.

But you're not stuck with just greens for a fresh-food item for your rabbit. Add to your shopping list minor quantities of other high-fiber foods like pears, peaches, apples, green or red bell peppers, mangoes, pineapples, pea pods and Brussels sprouts, and, once in a tiny while, a raisin or two. Offer these foods as treats, in tiny quan-tities when compared to the leafy greens. The higher levels of sugars and starches of sweet fruits end up being fermented by the normal bacteria in your rabbit's digestive tract.

Fruits are fine for a treat food; one of our local rabbit rescuers uses blueberries as a bribe when she's trying to persuade a new rabbit to come to her. High-fiber fruits like apples, pears, papayas, plums, and strawberries help keep the rabbit's gut doing what it should be doing. Papayas have an enzyme that anecdotally is supposed to break down the mucous coating of hairballs, theoretically making it easier to pass the hairball. You may hear of this beneficial effect from many people, but just nod and smile.

Avoid those fruits that are high in sugar, like grapes and bananas. I made an exception to this rule when my rabbit developed snuffles, and I just had to get the antibiotic into her twice a day. I mashed a bit of banana and stirred in the crushed antibiotic pills. Cleo gobbled up her medication every night and every morning.

Using treats

In training, the topic of treats will come up repeatedly. Treats are used as positive reinforcement, in that rabbit training for anything is best done as a positive action. It also makes training more fun, when your rabbit hops toward you, eyes

Play outside with your rabbit; he won't know he's being trained.

have your number, and they're willing to play it.

Pass on the brightly colored cereal mixtures, the yogurt-covered nuts, and the honey-coated mixes of sunflower seeds and puffed cereal. Your rabbit doesn't need sucrose or treats heavy in starches; keep in mind starches are processed in the rabbit's caecum, by the caecal bacteria, which give off gas as a by product. This leads to bloat and weight gain, hardly what you want for your rabbit.

Save those Cheerios or puffed rice for your breakfast table. Say "yes" to those treats that contain timothy, a single dried fruit or vegetable, or small chunks of fresh vegetables or fruits (carrots and apples may be the easiest to handle, since you can cut them up into small sticks for easy rewarding).

For packaged items, check the labels for their fat and carbohydrate content. Compare those figures to the gold standard of apple pieces or timothy hay. The treat my rabbits liked at first was a papaya mix, 12% protein, 3% fat, and 23% fiber. Apples in contrast are 1% protein, 0% fat, and 12% fiber.

To see what treats your bunny prefers (this week, that is) offer her a variety of treats, spread out on the floor in front of her and see which ones she picks up first. I fed my rabbits small carrots as part of their daily diet, and only after I starting training them did I realize that one of them absolutely adored paper clip-sized carrot sticks.

bright and ready to demonstrate what he knows. (Rather than treats as a steady rewards, work to make affection from you a reward. But to get you started, treats are a good way to reward behavior and establish a relationship.)

You can purchase many kinds of treats from your grocery store, pet store, a pet care catalog, or an online vendor. For packaged treats, read the labels to see exactly what you're buying. Treat manufacturers are very creative, and will add together amazing ingredients designed more to appeal to you, the owner, than to the rabbit. They

Chapter Three
Grooming

Rabbits groom each other as a comforting gesture and as a social action. Most often, one rabbit uses his tongue and lips to groom another by moving gently along the top of the head, the ears or the upper back.

When you groom your rabbit, there is a practical side: you make your rabbit look better and remove all that loose hair that otherwise ends up everywhere in your house. But there's an even more important part to grooming, and that is to strengthen the bond between the two of you.

Like other furred creatures, rabbits molt. Molting may occur one to four times a year, depending on the kind of rabbit you have, the temperature (when it goes from cold to warm or vice versa, get ready), and the diet. Molting only takes a couple of weeks to accomplish, but these weeks generally occur April through fall. Molting is most apparent on breeds with longer fur such as the Angora and the Jersey Wooly. Grooming also helps decrease the amount of hair your rabbit may inadvertently ingest.

For you and your rabbit, there are two types of grooming. One is social grooming, and it's more of a touching gesture than an actual tidy-up-that-coat gesture. This first type of grooming simply consists of taking the rabbit from its cage and petting it.

When you pet your rabbit, handle him. As he becomes more trusting over time, turn him over in your

"Since there's no one around me to help" . . .
A Netherlands Dwarf grooms himself.

A brush or a shedding comb will pick up loose hair before it leaves your rabbit.

fortable, and having your rabbit accustomed to this position will be helpful in other aspects of care, especially in giving medication or in nail clipping. It may take some time before you can do this; this is a very vulnerable position for a prey animal, and a nervous rabbit may kick out its legs in an attempt to right itself, resulting in a back fracture.

The other type of grooming is actual grooming, using your fingers, a comb, or a brush to clean and tidy up your rabbit's coat. Do this about once a week. You'd use your fingers primarily when you want to ease out the loose undercoat from an Angora or a Jersey Wooly. (This isn't painful to the rabbit; when the fur is ready to shed; it slips out in handfuls.) You use a brush as weekly maintenance on a short- or long-coated rabbit.

arms so he lies on his back. Hold him securely, just as you would a puppy or a human baby. Rabbits do not find this at all uncom-

Use grooming as an opportunity to talk to your rabbit as you check for any potential problems. Gently feel the rib area, for any tenderness or any lumps. Look at the feet for any evidence of sores on the back of the lower leg. Check under the chin area for any evidence of wet fur or inflammation. Check the ears for any possible damage from other rabbits (if you have them). Check out your rabbit's body for any unusual lumps or scaly spots on the skin. Let your fingers and your eyes tell you if there is anything that needs to be checked up on.

For simple grooming, you can keep your rabbit on your lap, or you

During quiet times, use your hands for social bonding and light grooming.

"Hmmm—Those ears could be a little cleaner." When it comes to good grooming, everyone has an opinion.

can put her on a countertop where you can easily hold her and restrain her if needed. As time goes by, your rabbit will enjoy the grooming so much you'll need to move her off your lap to let her know the session has ended.

Use a wire bristle brush, like a dog slicker brush, a softer brush like a cat brush or a human hairbrush, or a metal comb with rounded tips. The softer brushes work when not too much fur is being shed, and the comb works when your rabbit isn't shedding much at all.

Begin at the neck and gently brush or comb the rabbit's body, brushing or combing in the direction that the hair grows. You shouldn't find many tangled areas, unless your rabbit has longer fur than the mini-lops or the dwarf types. Don't spend more than a few minutes grooming the first few times, until your rabbit understands the routine and what's happening.

Long-haired breeds, particularly show angoras, are frequently groomed using a blower. There are commercial blowers, like leaf blowers but not nearly as noisy, that are self-standing and that blow room-temperature air out of a directional nozzle. You hold the rabbit on your lap or on a grooming table. With little brushing, the air gently blows apart tangled areas.

The downside of working with a blower is dealing with the fine hairs that are shed during the process and with the dander. Rabbits normally shed dander. If you use a blower inside, you are moving the dander off the surface of the

The Netherland Dwarf is a popular breed to keep as pets.

ners; most are happy to obtain fur from an animal that has been kept clean and if the fur has no mats. There are also schools and studios that teach spinning that might welcome your rabbit's fur. Magazines like *Spin-Off* and websites for spinning/weaving guilds) have classified ads for spinning supplies and fiber vendors. Angora is extremely fine and is usually combined with other fiber like lamb's wool or silk for spinning.

If all this fuss about shed fur seems a bit odd to you, you can just throw it away.

Nails

Check your rabbit's nails every month. You may need to trim them, unless your rabbit has a safe-foot area that wears her nails down, or unless she spends a lot of time out of her cage and runs in an area that will help wear the nails down. Pick up your rabbit and look at her feet. You'll note that she doesn't have footpads, poor thing, no rabbits do. Instead, they have quantities of fur, padding what you could call bony little toes.

Hold your rabbit on her back if she's used to it, or you can tuck her head between your arm and your body to help hold her in one place. Another method of holding a rabbit is on her back, in your lap, but with her head tucked between your knees. Rabbits seem quite calm and content if they can't see what's

skin onto the horizontal and vertical surfaces of the room. It gives an interesting aged-Gothic feel to the room. You'll inhale quantities of dander as well. (Wear a facemask if there's any chance you're allergic to rabbits.) If you use a blower, work outside so the dander powder won't add to your housekeeping chores.

What do you do with the fur your rabbit sheds? You can put the shed fur outside, for birds to nest with. If your rabbit is an angora, you can keep the plucked fur and spin the fiber into yarn yourself or give them to a weaver. Check in your local area for a yarn shop or an artisans' guild that might have spin-

Keep your rabbit's claws trimmed.

happening to them. Use a pair of nail clippers (either the guillotine-style sold for dog's nails or the side cutter style sold for cats will work equally well), and remove the tip of each nail. This is easy if the nail is light colored and you can see the vein running through it. If the nail is dark, take off just the sharp tip portion. If you do nick the vein, dab on a bit of baby powder or alum to stop the bleeding. Alum is marketed under several names, such as Stop-Quik, at your pet store. You can buy alum at your pharmacy; human males dab it on razor cuts. Alum is also sold seasonally in the canning supplies section at your local grocery store.

At the end of every grooming session or every nail-clipping session, take a moment to pet your rabbit and talk to her. If she gets frightened at any point, stop what you are doing and reassure her that nothing bad is going to happen to her. When you're done, put her back in her cage, down on the floor in your rabbit-proofed room, or back in her pen with a bit of a treat. You want every interaction with your rabbit to be a positive one.

Merlin has the ball – but will he push it back?

Chapter Four

Caging and Enrichment

Caging for house rabbits can be purchased or homemade. Other than cost, there's not much difference between the two, as long as you remember your rabbit needs room to stretch out and to move around, and that house rabbits do spend supervised time outside of their cage. At the minimum, the cage should be twice your rabbit's length when he is stretched out, and the cage width should be your rabbit's length, again when he is stretched out. A small Lop or Netherlands Dwarf rabbit measures about 18 inches (46 cm), flopped out, so his cage would be 18 inches wide and 36 inches long (46 × 91 cm), at a minimum. Larger breeds need proportionately larger cages.

You can buy a commercially made cage for your rabbit at a pet store. The larger stores have space to stock bulky supplies like rabbit cages, but smaller pet stores will be happy to order a cage for you. Your local feed store, in addition to selling rabbit hutches, may be able to order an indoor rabbit cage for you, but don't be surprised if you get asked, "You want to keep the rabbit inside, right?" as if no one has ever done this before. Check classified ads or Craigslist for a second-hand cage (Warning! Sometimes these cages come complete with rabbits.) You can buy very good cages online, and some of these

Commercial caging on casters can readily be moved to keep your rabbit with you.

are stackable units that are expandable into multistory cages.

Good cage designs have some commonalities that make a lot of sense. Make sure the cage has wire grid sides. Rabbits need the ventilation and the environmental stimulation that viewable wire sides provide. The cage should have at least a partial solid bottom. Because rabbits have no pads on their feet, they can develop a condition called sore hocks (although technically it is really sore ankles) if they have only a wire floor, or worse, if they are confined and must stand on their own waste. You can readily add a "foot safe" area by adding a rubber mat or a carpet square to a wire cage floor. There should be space for a litter box in the cage, because you want your rabbit to always use a litter box.

If your budget emits a clear "eek!" when you show it the nice cage you're thinking of buying, or if you just like making things, a homemade cage is simple and fairly easy. You can create an open-topped pen for your rabbit or an all-enclosed cage.

The open-topped pen is the easiest to set up and to keep clean. You can buy a portable dog exercise pen, which consists of multiple 2-foot-wide (24 cm) wire panels hinged together. You buy these pens by the height and the number of panels; one that will set up as a square, 4 feet (122 cm) on a side is a good basic size for a small to medium size rabbit.

Some commercial caging is little more than a wire box; plan for plenty of out-of-cage time.

Wire grid panels can be used for very serviceable cages. The panels are boxed as build-it-yourself storage cubes used in apartments and dorm rooms. Each grid measures 14 inches (36 cm) on a side. They are usually sold in packs of ten grids with snap-on connectors. Two packs, along with a package of plastic cable ties, will give you enough material for a pen, 2 grids high and 10 grids long, large enough to sit on top of a 3 × 4 foot (91 × 122 cm) piece of carpet to create a small indoor pen.

Most people use 1-inch binder clips or dog leash clips to provide an easy-open, easy-close pen. I

umed or spot cleaned. They provide secure footing for a rabbit that wishes to hop around or stand on his hind legs for a treat.

Other flooring choices include area carpets, the washable kind, woven grass mats, and plastic screening over newspapers. Area carpets provide good footing, but their absorbent nature means frequent washing, and the backing doesn't hold up well to repeated washings. The lightweight grass floor mats come in varying sizes, but the usual is 3 × 6 feet (91 × 183 cm). These are inexpensive, easy to store and shake out, but you can't wash or vacuum them, and they are not durable. You can buy smaller, grass mats designed for rabbits to chew upon and rest upon.

Heavy-duty sliding door screening—called "pet screening"—from my local big box home improvement store worked really well for flooring. Pet screening comes in 4-foot (122 cm) widths. Laid down over several layers of newspaper, this provides secure footing that will absorb most moisture problems. It is also a barrier that can be swept or vacuumed. Every week or so, take up the screening and replace the newspaper. This screening also works directly on top of a vinyl floor for rabbits that are good with their litter boxes. It provides the traction they need to hop around.

used binder clips until I found my rabbit would pick up the caging in his teeth and bang it up and down until the binder clips would jiggle off. Instant freedom for rabbit.

Flooring for the pen can be obtained from a variety of sources. You do want to provide some sort of traction for your rabbit's feet. The easiest to use is door mats from your local home improvement store. These can be taken outside and hosed off when they become dirty. Buy the largest mat that will fit under the pen area; the 3 × 4-foot (91 × 122 cm) carpet door mats with a flat rubber edge lay flat, are waterproof, and can be easily vacu-

If an enclosed cage is more what you want, you can make one using the grids and cable ties. Overlap the grids when you don't want to use the full 14-inch (36 cm) width. The grids you designate for the door panel set need to be about 1 inch larger all the away around than the door opening, to give more structural integrity to the door. When it comes to cage flooring, most rabbit keepers put in a wire mesh floor, using 14 or 16 gauge welded wire with a $\frac{1}{2} \times 1$ inch grid. You can instead put the cage itself down into a solid wooden flooring unit with 2-inch raised sides, and simply lift the cage out of the bottom to clean the litter box and the cage floor.

Heavyweight pet screening (right) is much more durable than regular screening (left) for pen flooring.

Other caging necessities

Add to the pen or cage a hide box for your rabbit, a water bowl or drip water bottle (a bottle with an angled spout, just like you've seen used for rat cages), a food bowl, a rabbit litter box, a holder for the hay, and a few toys.

Adding a second rabbit

European rabbits are above all social creatures. They live together in groups of 20 to 150 in the wild in underground warrens. The inter-connected passageways have rabbit-sized rooms at intervals, so although the rabbits live together, they have access to "alone" time.

Domesticated rabbits are accustomed to human caretakers, but

Bonded rabbits will sit together and groom each other—but this doesn't let you off the grooming hook.

Tim checks out the clown pants, sold as a hiding place for cats.

this doesn't mean there's any less need for company, meaning other rabbits. Studies of lab and house rabbits show there are more natural behaviors and fewer ritualistic behaviors (like excessive licking and apathetic staring) in rabbits kept with a companion rabbit. A study in Sweden showed that house rabbits kept singly have half the life span of a rabbit kept with a companion.

Rabbits kept with a companion rabbit have someone they can relate to 24 hours a day, another rabbit to sit with (bookend-fashion), to take care of grooming needs, to play with, to eat with, and to sleep with. We humans can try, but we can't fill the need a companion rabbit can fill.

Most caretakers work outside the home and are gone anywhere from 4 to 10 hours a day. That's a long time to leave a house rabbit by himself, even in the nicest cage;

toys and filled food containers are a distraction, but they can't provide the mental and emotional stimulation that another rabbit can provide, effortlessly.

But don't rush out and get a second rabbit and expect Rabbit A to get along with Rabbit B. Rabbits just don't generally love each other right off. In fact, strangers-to-each-other rabbits usually argue and can injure each other via biting and grab-and-kicking.

You can get around this natural proclivity if you have access to a pool of second-rabbit candidates. Start with your local rabbit rescue. They know the rabbits in their care, who is mellow and who is not.

The get-acquainted process begins with a supervised introduction, first in adjoining pens and, if that works, in a co-joined pen. It's considered a match if the rabbits end up lying next to each other and, ideally, grooming each other. It's not a match if they run at each other and start tearing fur out, but you would have figured that out.

Barring an accessible supply of second rabbits, two strangers-to-each-other rabbits may learn to get along if kept in adjoining cages until they learn to ignore each other. Then they can be given supervised time together in multiple sessions until it's clear that no aggression exists. I would like to say this method works with most rabbits, but be prepared to be patient and understand that some rabbits may never learn to get along. Also, be prepared for urine and droppings to be deposited as close as possible to the other rabbit's cage, even if both are neutered/spayed. It's just a territory thing.

Cage enrichment

You've got to admit, there's not much to look at in a cage. Rabbits need stimulation or they become apathetic. On their own, outside, where they can choose where they go and what they do, rabbits are playful, resourceful creatures. They'll try to play with almost anything. Rabbits in the home need cage enrichment, items they can play with and manipulate.

Cage enrichment simply means offering a changing environment to a caged animal. Zoo keepers do this with the creatures in their care, and the keepers know that enrichment doesn't just mean a couple

Cut rings from a paper towel tube to make a chewable, tossable toy.

of toys. Enrichment is richer than that. It can mean moving the rabbit to a different cage on weekends, perhaps into an outside pen for a couple of hours. Enrichment can be sensory, meaning changes in the visual, olfactory, tactile, or taste elements in the cage. Typical sensory changes for your rabbits would include changing cage toys, adding a section of Astro turf carpeting or a soft pillow, or tossing in branches from a pear tree (very tasty).

Enrichment techniques include feeding changes, either by offering different food items or by providing the opportunity for an animal to "work" for its food. Zoos add an activity for their bears by secreting food items in designed hiding spots in their cage. There are toys you can buy that require a flat disc to be moved before the treat is revealed. You can also hide treats under small overturned baskets

Lightweight toys can be used for cage enrichment and for instructing "Touch" and "Push." These items were purchased from a thrift shop.

or in small bowls that will conceal what is within. I used plastic peanut butter jar lids and found my rabbits had little trouble finding and over-turning the right lid: flip! chomp! So much for that technique.

Enrichment includes time with other animals. Interactions with new animals must be monitored. This is where you teach your rabbit and another rabbit to live together or to co-exist in the same household with dogs/cats.

Enrichment also refers to small items—safe toys—the animals can manipulate.

Additionally, enrichment means training. Training is a form of socialization with humans. In zoos, training means making medical examinations less stressful for the animal and veterinarian. For rabbits, training will give you a rabbit that readily uses her litter box, runs to the front of her cage when some-one approaches, and puts both front feet forward to touch human hands when asked to "gimme five." This type of enrichment helps elimi-nate boredom and removes the fear from contact with humans.

Enrichment for rabbits doesn't have to cost an arm and a leg. You can do a lot with items you already have around the house. Rabbits like to chew, so provide items they can safely chew on. Think of offer-ing a variety of small cardboard boxes, unpainted wooden shims, and other items to chew on, such as cut branches from a citrus or apple tree. Offer unpainted baskets,

Trained agility rabbits get to go places and do things. Wallaby pauses on the bunny walk (with the help of his handler).

blocks of untreated lumber, or one of those inch-thick woven grass door mats from a home improvement store.

Look at the toys in the parrot section of your pet store—most of them have chewable, movable pieces that can be moved around. The baby section of your grocery store has hard plastic toys, like plastic keys or interlocking rings, that are lightweight and almost indestructible.

Your kitchen may have some items that would work. My rabbits looked at the array of cardboard tubes with evident distain, but maybe your rabbits would like the brands you buy. Try an empty soda can with a few pebbles inside and the opening taped over.

Offer your rabbit(s) a digging place by providing a cardboard box with an inch or so of newspaper laid in the bottom. Go to Goodwill and buy a half dozen small stuffed toys (If they have glued-on plastic eyes or plastic noses, remove them so your rabbit won't swallow them).

You don't have to spend a lot of money; the goal is to provide objects your rabbits can manipulate, meaning objects they can chew on or toss around.

Time out!

One of the biggest enrichments you can provide your rabbits—and at essentially no cost—is time out of his cage. House rabbits are lit-

Chewable parrot toys work for bunnies, too.

erally rabbits that run around the house or at the least a room that has been altered slightly to make it safe for the rabbit. Most rabbit keepers I know give their rabbits house time every day.

There are some precautions you'll need to take. Rabbits are chewers, so anything that is chewable, such as phone wires or electrical cords or the pull cords for draperies or even the wooden legs of tables or desks, need to be protected from the rabbit's teeth. Your rabbit doesn't chew when she's

Even a trained rabbit will nibble on electrical cords, so pull them out of the way of temptation.

½- or ¾-inch clear plastic tubing at your local big box hardware store, and split it down its length. Slide it over the plug end of your phone cords and electrical cords.

You can rabbit-proof a room by barricading off the forbidden areas. I used a series of those versatile 14-inch (36 cm) grid panels, fastened together by twist-ties and leaned against the wall with the electrical socket, to block my computer cords away from my bunny's curiosity. I was always in that room when my bunny was loose, so any effort of his part to move the grid system was met with a "no, no" and a distraction.

out of her cage, you say? Do not think that just because your rabbit has never sampled the wire that hangs down from the back of your printer that she won't try it, ever. She will. For those cords you can't keep tucked behind something, buy

Leave the door of the cage open while your rabbit enjoys her "free" time. Enjoy interacting with your rabbit during these times. Don't be surprised when she hops up to you and puts her paws on your leg. Tickle her head and toss a small ball for her. When you're ready for her to go back in her cage, tell her it's time to go home, and put one of her favorite foods just inside her cage. She can learn to go back into her cage on command; that's part of what you will learn in this book. First, you may need to pick her up and put her back in her cage, or herd her gently toward the cage. You want her to enjoy coming out of her cage and to be happy to go back into it.

You can buy chewable woven grass mats to provide a foot-safe area.

Chapter Five
Talking Rabbit

Your rabbit speaks first

Training your rabbit will be easier and more rewarding if you first learn your rabbit's language. Rabbits, both wild and domestic, speak with body language. Body postures, ear positions, and physical actions all reveal bunny emotions. If you know what your rabbit is saying to you, you can tailor your response, and training will proceed much more comfortably.

Some of your rabbit's expressions are confined to a single body part. A single emotion, for example, may be expressed via the ears or the body position. More often, however, they are combined, as when a head shake is combined with a foot flick. We'll start with the bunny head and work backward from there.

Head positions

Head flick. When your rabbit flicks his head to the side, not just an ear shake, but uses his entire head, he's saying "Hey, I see you and I like you. Do you like me/want to play?" Your response must be a head flick of your own, as if you're tossing your hair out of your eyes. Get down on the ground and offer your rabbit something to play with. If you prefer, you can leap around for a few minutes to indicate your general happiness with the situation, but my rabbits never seemed to respond to my antics.

Albus speaks of his happiness by performing a binkie.

A rabbit's face and actions speak for him.

Head nudge. You may be sitting at your desk, feeding yourself something tasty like crackers and minding your own business, when suddenly you feel a distinct nudge from your house rabbit's nose. You look down and there she is, at your feet, looking at you soulfully with those big bunny eyes. The nudge is a request for petting or a request for treats. Bunnies can be shameless beggars for either, and it's a close contest as to which they prefer. What is one to do? Give in, of course. Give him a gentle scuffling of the hair between his eyes and his ears; tell him to sit up, and offer something green and crunchy or maybe a piece of carrot when he puts his little rump down and reaches up with his nose. See, you've got him trained already.

The "say again?" wince. A rabbit that can't figure out your actions may react with a quick one-eyed wink and a facial wince. Like the human facial expressions studies done by psychologist Paul Ekman, this fast-flicker of emotion is easy to miss but nonetheless important. Your rabbit is telling you he doesn't understand what you are saying. Slow down, rethink what you're trying to communicate, and try again.

Active sniffing. Rabbits use their noses all the time to find out what's going on. The exaggerating nose sniffing indicates an almost-aroused interest, meaning a bunny who is calm and probably lying on its side in complete abandonment to relaxation has realized the scent may be something worth getting up for. The nose will tell her.

Even when relaxed, a rabbit's nose is active.

A slow wiggle may indicate contentment, which is a nice condition. The speed of the sniffing will increase if the scent is worth noticing. Is it food? Could it mean danger? If the nose message is impressive enough, the rabbit may stop snuffling and use her eyes and ears to check things out. You may wish to make some loud, slow sniffing sounds yourself to tell her that there is nothing to worry about.

Chinning. When you first let your house rabbit out of his pen or cage to explore his new home, after a few minutes of hopping around, you may see him running his chin over the vertical portions of your rolling office chair or along the side of your trash can. This isn't a new form of Braille, it's a chemical marking process called chinning. Rabbits claim objects and surfaces in their caging or enclosure by chinning. This places an odorless mark (odorless to humans, at least) on the object. The scent is exuded by scent glands along the bottom of the jaw line. Other bunnies may come that way and will need to know there's already a bunny in residence. Be complimented if your rabbit chins you, and be grateful for this chemical communication system. (Rabbits also use urine to communicate, but more about that on page 43.)

"Purring." When you are sitting with your rabbit or perhaps carrying her from one place to another, you may be startled when she makes a soft sound that sounds just like

A rabbit will chin items in his realm to claim them.

teeth chattering or if you were taking multiple small bites from a carrot, using only your front teeth. This is called rabbit purring. It sounds nothing like a kitten's purr. But it does indicate rabbit contentment, and it's a good thing to hear if you are petting or holding a rabbit.

Ear positions

Ears are a good barometer as to your rabbit's state of mind. Ear messages are often paired with other parts of the body, of course, so start with the ears and then look at the rest of the body.

Curious. When your rabbit is curious about something, he'll lean forward, with ears facing forward, and his body will be balanced on his front legs. He may waggle his ears around like antennas, to see

Is this floor slippery everywhere? A bunny makes sure his footing is secure.

what extra info he can pick up before he actually moves forward. Reward him for his curiosity. Give him a treat.

Rabbits use active sniffing to find out what's going on.

Nervous. If your rabbit has both ears with the openings down but extended wide like antennae, yet she isn't leaning forward, or if her body is partially turned in case she needs to flee, she's nervous about something. She's trying to be inconspicuous until she finds out what is going on. If her ears have the openings turned down toward the ground, and her body is crouched down and turned partially away from you, she's flat-out scared.

Mixed emotions. When one ear faces backward and the other forward, your rabbit hasn't quite decided how he feels. He's not quite happy with you or perhaps it is his situation. If he isn't facing you, or if he turns his back on you with both of his ear openings tilted down, he is not happy. Something needs to be fixed.

Anger. A rabbit that moves her ears from the happy alert position to facing out to the sides is getting irritated. The next step is to swivel the ears so the opening faces backward while the ears are tilted up vertically. The tail may be extended out straight away from the body (yes, the tail speaks as well), while the legs are held apart and erect as if the bunny is ready to move and move quickly. When the ears move again to press back against the body with the openings down, move back, give the rabbit her space, and make some appeasement gestures, either by speaking or by grooming yourself. This is an upset bunny.

Some rabbits do have aggression issues. Unaltered males tend to be more aggressive than males that have been neutered. Aggression by a rabbit of either sex may be due in part how that rabbit was handled (if at all) before you got her. Aggressive bunnies take a lot of extra time when it comes to training, but they do respond. Treat them kindly, always.

The body in motion

Thumping. Probably the first message you ever received from your rabbit was a loud thump when he was startled or when he went back into his cage after being handled. The loud thump is made by both of the back feet or a single hind foot being smacked once or twice against the floor.

Enough! A Dutch bunny speaks with his feet—he leaves.

Thumping has two messages, both warnings. The thump is used to tell intruders—such as you—that you stepped over the line, behaviorwise. Thumping can also be used as a type of seismic communication, like the ultra-deep rumble elephants use to communicate over distances. It's a warning signal for any other rabbits within range that something's not quite right.

Turning away. Another indication that you've just gone too far is the indignant back turn. Your rabbit may do this the first few times you handle her. She'll hop into her house and turn her back, or she'll just take one hop away and turn her back on you. Sometimes she'll look back over her shoulder to see if you're paying attention, then she'll turn her face resolutely to the wall. If she could sing she'd be singing loudly "I can't hear you lalalala." This is particularly common when you and the rabbit

A rabbit comforts himself by grooming.

haunches and hold his front feet in front of him with the bottom sides of the paws clasped together. He'll clean his paws first, before any facial grooming takes place. He cleans the bristly hair on the bottom of his feet with quick licks of his tongue, and will nibble-clean the claw area. Then he'll use fast licks to clean the upper sides of his front paws. Now it's time for the face.

While his paws are still damp, he will use the bristly hair on the bottoms to brush the hair on his face forward. Facial cleaning usually begins with the eye area and the eyelids. Your rabbit will turn his head as he rubs his paws down his face to make certain all areas are brushed clean. Then he'll work on the ears, using his paws to push the ears forward, toward his mouth, so he can clean the lower part of his ears with his mouth (this is easier if he's a lop or if he has long ears). He'll clean his paws again, pull his ears down and clean them with quick strokes of his paws, always stroking with the direction of the fur.

Some rabbit keepers feel they can make their rabbit more comfortable by miming grooming. Just look at your rabbit and when you see him looking at you, mime his grooming actions. Pretend to lick your hands with special attention to your nails. Wipe your palms over the orbits of your eyes. Smooth back your hair on both sides of your face and brush over your ears. Pretend to clean your hands again and

are new to each other. This isn't personal; it is temporary, providing you don't give up. Speak softly and put a treat near her.

Turning and the Foot Flick. If the back turn is followed by the bunny hopping away from you and flicking her hind feet as if she's just stepped in water or something nastier, the gesture means she wants to get rid of something.

Grooming. When you put your rabbit back in his cage, she may take a few minutes to put herself right by grooming. Grooming is used as self-assurance and as a bonding tool (rabbits groom each other as a gesture of affection).

A rabbit placed in an uncomfortable situation will tidy up once he feels safe. He will sit on his

wipe the sides of your face. Then offer your rabbit a treat.

Grooming another rabbit is a bonding gesture and usually takes place after a few perfunctory strokes of self grooming. Rabbits tend to begin grooming another rabbit by gentle grooming nibbles along the edges of the ears, followed by gentle licking around the eyes.

Offer to groom your rabbit by putting your hand down flat on the ground in front of him. Move the fingers to scratch up the ground slightly. If he moves forward and lowers his head, your offer has been accepted.

Begin the grooming with gentle tickles between the eyes or gentle stroking along the ears and back. Keep in mind that both of you will have to get used to this grooming process, because it isn't going to feel the same as grooming by another rabbit. (Generally speaking, physical contact by another species is not usually a "safe" experience for a rabbit.) Be patient and consistent and gentle. Ask him if he'd like a bit of a tickle, and offer a small treat at the end of your first few grooming sessions as a reward for allowing you to impinge on his space.

Periscoping. When a rabbit wants to see what's going on in an area not immediately next to her, she may try periscoping. Like a small child who stands on tippy toe to look over a fence, the periscoping rabbit balances on her hind legs

Timmy periscopes to see what's going on.

and rump, elongates her torso and tips her head back ever so slightly to see what is down the road a bit. She's just curious. Tell her to "sit up" and reward her with a carrot bit.

Binkies. Happy bunnies that have enough room like to run in big circles. They will leap into the air and kick their hind legs sideways in gyrations called "binkies." They are the sign of a happy rabbit who is saying "Wheee! Look at me!" Some owners run in circles and binky back at their rabbits. Try this only if your back is agile.

Happy circling. A rabbit that runs in circles around your feet is enjoying the space he has to run. The gesture is also used by male rabbits who are courting their love object, in this case, you. Sometimes this circular running is just a shameless bid for attention, so lean down and pet your rabbit. Next time he circles, ask him if he loves you and reward him with a treat.

Holding your rabbit. Picking up your rabbit heralds a new series of body statements. The most obvious is kicking, and your rabbit is just telling you she doesn't like to be picked up. Instead of holding her in front of you like a struggling volleyball, shift her to the one-arm carry. Bend your elbow so your forearm lies along your body with your hand somewhere near your navel. The bunny should be lying atop your forearm, nose nestled between your elbow and your body, and your hand of that arm cupped firmly around her rump. She can't kick her way out of your grasp with this

hold. This hold is harder if you're a petite person holding a medium-sized rabbit, but it is possible. Alternatively, you can pick her up with two hands, sit down in a soft chair or on your sofa, and put her on your lap, with one hand held loosely over her shoulders so she can't leap off your lap. No matter which carry you use, hold onto your rabbit firmly and be careful of those slender leg bones.

Rabbits do learn to enjoy being held, and they will run to their owners and ask to be petted. But you may meet another bunny owner who doesn't think bunnies should be picked up and held, ever. Some bunny owners believe a pet rabbit belongs on the floor and should not be held for any reason. It's certainly possible to be a good bunny owner and never pick up your rabbit. The trainers I've met are ready to hold (and shower with affection) their bunnies.

The messages of droppings

Rabbits, and wild rabbits in particular, use their droppings as signal devices. Outdoor rabbits tend to drop them sort of willy-nilly all over their site (this says "my space" pretty clearly if you're a rabbit). They also deposit their droppings in shallow trenches, sometime communally, that mark the boundaries of their pen or territory. The build-

Touch your rabbit before you pick him up.

A litter box with high sides will keep rabbit rumps inside the box.

up of odor from these stockpiled feces serves as a clearly discernable warning of territory limits to any rabbits from another warren. Rabbits who venture beyond these visual and olfactory warnings may be attacked or chased away by the rabbits of the home warren.

From a human standpoint, the piled up feces are much easier to shovel up and place on a mulch pile or dump in flowerbeds—they are a great nitrogen source. But for an inside rabbit and most particularly for a house rabbit, it is important to get the message across fairly quickly that the litter box is the place for urine and droppings (see page 44).

Urine is also used as a signal device. Male rabbits that have not been neutered will mark their territory by spraying (as will females, but to a much lesser extent). Having your pet altered will greatly decrease this sort of signaling, and adding a barricade to side of the litter box will prevent oversprays.

Chapter Six
Training

Getting your rabbit to come to you

Having your rabbit come when called is so basic. It is also one of the starting blocks in training.

You begin by sitting on the floor with your rabbit, holding something

Training a rabbit to sit up is one of the easiest tricks.

wonderful in your hands, food-wise. Talk to your rabbit and scratch your fingers on the floor in front of you, bunny-speak for "would you like me to groom you?" Tell your rabbit "Come!" using his name. Reward him when he hops up to you, even if it takes a few minutes. Praise him and pat him as well. Let him hop away, and after a minute or two, repeat the command and reward him when he comes to you. Give the command and reward him even if he hops by you by accident; you want him to associate the command with coming up to you and being rewarded.

Litter box training

Litter box training may be the easiest training you'll ever do with your rabbit. It consists of two steps:

1. Placing the litter box where you'd like your rabbit to use it and, ultimately,

2. Placing another litter box where your rabbit decides to go.

This second step is particularly important when your bunny becomes a real house rabbit.

The first step means you put a litter box in a corner of your rabbit's cage. Since the first cage is often pretty small, perhaps as small as 20 × 30 inches (51 × 76 cm), there's not a lot of hopping around room for your rabbit. Chances are your rabbit will recognize the box for what it is and will readily use it. Rabbits are by nature tidy creatures that use one corner of a warren chamber for defecation. Domestic rabbits, honed in part by selective breeding, will generally seek and use one spot regularly, and the clean litter box seems to invite defecation and urination. The even-better news is that once they recognize a litter box as their personal toilet, you can move the box around in a larger cage and they'll still use it. The key is to clean the litter box every three days or however frequently needed, and this means you pick up the litter box, dump the contents and refill it with clean litter. Your rabbit gets nose-to-nose with it on a regular basis and he knows when it needs cleaning.

You may find your rabbit uses his litter box but continues to sprinkle droppings around his cage. This is a marking technique that simply claims the area as his. You can understand that he doesn't want any interlopers moving into his turf. You'd feel the same if a stranger set up his space in your living room (marking isn't really an option for you). Just sweep up the rabbit droppings and drop them into the litter box. Since they are dry, round

Two litter boxes are better than one.

and have little apparent odor, this is a quick and easy action.

"Dropping sprinkling" becomes more pronounced the more rabbits you put together. When you have more than three rabbits, the dropping process seems to turn into a contest, with every rabbit convinced the area belongs to him and claiming the area with his droppings. You'll "win" this battle if you frequently sweep up the droppings.

You have many choices as far as litter box design goes. You can use a commercial cat litter box, but they take a lot of litter and reek when they get dirty. The commercially made high-backed corner litter boxes that are smaller are better suited for a single dwarf rabbit. The

You can make a temporary litter box from a cardboard box lined with plastic shelf paper.

smaller litter boxes hold very little litter and need to be cleaned every other day or so. The larger ones are deeper, and some have a grid that clicks into place over the litter. You could also use a plastic shoe box.

Ready to go outside — leash training makes walks enjoyable.

If you are worried about your rabbit hanging her fuzzy butt over the edge of the box and defecating or urinating onto the cage floor, put a plastic insert between the litter box and the side of the cage. Plastic page protectors with thin cardboard inside work well, or you can go to a print shop and have thin cardboard sheets laminated with their 5 mil laminate. I made urine shields made from pages of an old rabbit calendar that I laminated. The photos make me smile when I clean the rabbit cages.

A note about litters: It makes a difference what kind of litter you use. Do not use clumping litters, the aromatic wood shaving litters, the aromatic crystal litters or a corn cob litter. Rabbits' habit of dining on cecotropes directly from the anus means occasional litter ingestion, and the litters listed above could be fatal.

Recycled newspaper litters and compressed pine sawdust litters are on the list of "good" litters.

Leash training

Leash training is useful if you want to take your rabbit outside or if you want to compete in rabbit agility or jumping. Having your bunny on a leash provides you with some control over her while you're waiting for your spot in a competition or in case the two of you are outdoors and a loud sound sends her into a complete panic.

The right harness and leash

Start with a standard 6-foot (2 m) lightweight leash and a halter that is sized to fit your rabbit. A harness gives you control over your rabbit without putting his delicate bones, particularly his neck, at risk. Just measure around your bunny's neck, then under his arms and around his body, and take those measurements to your pet store. For my rabbit, a dignified 10-pound (4.5 kg) New Zealand White doe with a prominent dewlap, the neck and body/armpit measurements were the same.

You can use a harness made for a small dog or cat, or you may be able to find a rabbit harness. There are three harness designs to select from. All of these harness styles allow you to fit the neck and body portions to your rabbit.

One design is the figure 8 harness, with one loop around the neck and the other around the body. The leash clips to a ring at the junction of the two adjustable loops.

Another harness style is an H harness, with two separate neck and chest loops connected with a strap. The leash clips to the junction of the strap and the larger back loop.

The third style is a mesh or fabric harness. The middle of the mesh hourglass fits between your bunny's front legs, against his chest, and the extended ends of each end of the hourglass fit around the neck and the body. The leash clips to a ring at the juncture of the hourglass ends. The advantage to the mesh harness is that there's no pressure of straps against your bunny's body.

When you get the harness home, fit the harness onto your rabbit. There should be room for you to put one finger between the harness and the animal's body, once you get the harness fastened. Hold him and pet him for a few minutes. You want him to begin early on to associate the harness with being petted and other wonderful things. Let him run around with the harness on, so he can get used to the feel. Stay with him, like small children, bunnies can get into trouble with things that seem to be harmless.

It is not unusual for a bunny to find a harness uncomfortable at first. He may do the jump and shimmy; he may dash into his house and try to dislodge the harness. Another treat or two may be in order.

After 10 minutes or so with the harness on, take it off. Repeat the harness process at least once a day for four or five days, then put a lightweight leash on the harness and let your rabbit hop around a bit, trailing the leash. You are there, to make sure he doesn't get tangled up in anything and to offer praise and treats.

Suited up in her mesh harness, Maddie takes on the world.

At the outset, let me point out that walking on a leash as we would define it (the bunny follows our lead and moves where we wish to go) is not normal bunny behavior. When you are willing to redefine "walking on a leash" as getting your bunny to accept a harness and leash and for her to hop around an area while you hold the other end of the leash and follow her around, you have something you can train your bunny to do.

All you have to do is to harness her, add the leash, put her down and let her nose around for a while before she begins to explore. Don't attempt to pull her in the direction you want to go. It isn't going to work, and it is only going to upset her. You can use the leash to stop her from entering a dangerous area, and you'll have to scoop her up in your arms to physically relocate her.

Try to select a cement area or a driveway for these initial sessions. A green/grassy area offers the distraction of food. You can almost see your bunny thinking "Is that plant good to eat? Maybe I should try it. Oh maybe not, let me go for that green spiky thing to my left. No, wait, maybe I'd just rather sit a moment and look around."

With more and more training sessions, your bunny will get to the point where she really enjoys these times outside. At that point, you can try to train her to walk with you.

Hershey dubiously inspects his new harness.

It will take using treats as a lure and multiple short training sessions to help her understand what you'd like her to do. Be prepared for partial or intermittent success. Some rabbits seem to understand a training concept perfectly but seem to decide that's not something they are interested in doing today.

Interestingly enough, once a bunny has begun training for agility or jumping competitions, she tends to be better with a leash, because wearing the leash means something fun is going to happen.

Don't be surprised if your house rabbit clambers up to look out a window.

Tricks

It always amazes people how readily a rabbit can be trained to do simple commands.

If you spend part of your time sitting on a sofa or chair, reading or watching TV, invite your rabbit to join you. Call her over to you, or wait until she hops over to you and stands on his hind legs to see what you're doing. Pick her up and place her beside you and give the command "Up." It took my rabbit less than a week to find out that "Up" meant more petting and time out of the cage. (Don't be surprised if your rabbit remembers how to jump onto your sofa when you're not in the room and checks behind the cushions for stray bits of food. Rabbits find that humans tend to stash food in odd places like that.) Conversely, when you're ready to have your rabbit out of your lap, place

her on the floor and give the command "Down."

Part of your goal in training your rabbit to spend her time near you is to reinforce the bond between you. To paraphrase a popular song, you want her to want to be with you.

The command "No" will be useful to stop any undesired behavior, and rabbits are quite good at retaining what this means. This does not mean they will obey; they will just know what you're talking about. If your rabbit is doing something he ought not to—like dragging your purse to a spot where it could be investigated more thoroughly without interruption—you say "No! No!" (and remove the purse). Offer him a treat. All training needs to be oriented toward pleasure, not punishment. If it's easier to remove the rabbit from the temptation rather

House rabbits need supervision because everything is interesting and possibly worth nibbling on.

than vice versa, perhaps because he's chewing on floor molding, give the command "No! No!" and scoop him up gently, pet him a bit and put him down somewhere else. It will only take a few times until your rabbit decides that getting caught chewing on floor molding gets him

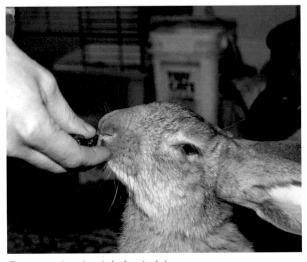

Ben accepts a treat during training.

moved away from his treasure. He will stop chewing on the molding when you're around. This is another reason why rabbits need to be under supervision when they are out of their cages.

At the end of your training session together, put your rabbit back into her cage. Use a command to go with the action, so your rabbit will learn what's expected of her. Amy Spintman of the San Diego House Rabbit Society uses "Dinner!" and her rabbits rush back into their cage to get food. Joanna Campbell, a house rabbit educator and fosterer from Minneapolis uses "Bedtime." I used the word "bedtime" to summon my rabbits when it was time for them to go back in their cages. Since the cages were already on the floor and the doors were open, I trained my rabbits by shooing them toward their cages with the command "Bedtime!" I added some greens or another treat to the cage before I ushered them inside, and I was simply persistent. After a week or so, they'd look at me when I gave the command, and then would hop back to their cages and go inside. This command was especially useful when they were in their outdoor pen and it was time for them to come back indoors. I kept a plastic cat carrier in the pen, lined with newspaper. It made a nice snoozing spot during the day. I'd enter the pen, toss a few greens in the cat carrier, and give the command "Bedtime." They'd hop toward the carrier and go inside.

Sometimes they'd short-circuit the process by using the carrier as a resting spot. All I had to do was to pick it up and close the door.

Sit up: Hold a favorite treat over your bunny's head so he will have to reach up to get it. Give the command "Sit up." When he stands on his hind legs to take the treat, praise him. This may take only a few tries until your bunny knows what the command means. When he spots the treat in your hand and hears the command, he'll know what to do.

Turn around: Hold the treat near your bunny's face so he can see it. When he reaches for it, give the command "Turn around" and literally lead him in a circle with the treat. When he completes the circle, give him his treat and praise him. This is another trick that your rabbit may pick up quickly.

Give me five: this exercise will make your bunny seem like the smartest rabbit in the world. Begin by sitting on the floor with your rabbit, with the treat in your fingers, palm up. Put your hand down on the ground in front of him, fingers up, where he can actually see the treat. When he touches your hand, tell him "Give me five" and release the treat. When he catches on that he has to touch your fingers with his paws in order to get the treat, flatten your hand so it lies on the floor, palm up. Give the command "Give me five." When he touches your hand with his paws, reward him.

Eliminating bad behaviors

Biting. You've got a nice new rabbit, but she's no baby. Maybe it's a foster rabbit; maybe you acquired it permanently from a-friend-of-a-friend.

In any case, you aren't really sure where this rabbit has been or what she's seen, but one thing you've found out is that she nips. You walk up to the cage, all friendliness and light, open the door and reach in, talking nicely all the while. Your rabbit eyes you, hops over, and gives you a brisk nip, hard enough to draw blood.

You have been given a message, as clearly as your rabbit can speak. It's just that right now you're slow on the uptake.

I know you bought the cage she's in. I know you picked out the dishes and the food and the very

Consistent, gentle treatment will change a nipper into a nuzzler.

hay lining her litter pan. That was then, this is now. All that stuff now belongs to the rabbit. You started this event by sticking your big fat hand right into her space. If a giant hairy hand came groping at you through your front door you probably wouldn't have the presence of mind to even offer a tiny nip. At least your rabbit's mind doesn't go blank at moments of panic, and her gesture was not really personal. She's just telling you to go away.

What you need to do is to work on your relationship with this rabbit, the same way you would with a rabbit that doesn't nip. The guidelines are the same. Put her cage where she'll see you when you're at home. Talk to her whenever you go by the cage. Give her a treat when she comes to the front of her cage when you walk by. Pick her up gently and talk to her, and pet her. She needs to lose her fear of you.

When you open the cage, let your rabbit come to you. If you're too impatient to recite the preamble of the Constitution while you wait for your rabbit to come to you (it takes time for her to decide you are notice-worthy), sweeten the approach. Make an opened cage door a sign of good things to come. Put in a few raisins. Talk to her. Offer a new bunch of hay. Usually the nipping is more of a cage-

guarding mechanism than an overt aggression toward you.

Don't hesitate to handle her, at least once a day, and talk to her while you handle her. Carry her around the house and show her items around the house. "This is the refrigerator, where we keep your lettuce. See, the door comes open and look what I found! A bit of lettuce." Talk to her. You need to reeducate your rabbit into enjoying being handled, and into enjoying being with you. If she does nip you, let out a sharp "Yeow!" and continue to handle her. Sit down on the floor and play with her, or rather, let her show you how to play. Give her toys to toss around. One of my rabbits loved to pounce on a narrow strip of newspaper trailed temptingly in front of him. Another rabbit was fascinated by the sound of a rolling bell, originally a bird's toy. My pair of rescue rabbits (only one of which bit me) loved tearing into a paper bag that had been folded over.

It doesn't take all that long. Within a few days, the beautiful gray and brown nipping rabbit became a gentle creature, hopping hesitantly up to me when I opened the cage and closing her eyes as I gently tickled the top of her head. You can do this with your rabbit. All it takes is time and your patience.

Chapter Seven
Clicker Training

Clicker training is a positive reinforcement program in which you'll use a clicker to reinforce a desired action. Good behavior gets a click (and a treat, in the beginning). Undesired behavior is ignored. Your goal is to make training such a pleasant experience for your bunny that he'll work for the reward and the treat, and soon for the clicker sound alone. It's that simple. You will be shaping your rabbit's behavior with the help of a clicker, while your rabbit will begin to look at training sessions as sort of a game (can you say enrichment?), where his actions gain him a reward.

What's so great about clicker training? The sound serves as instant reinforcement. It's feedback, and it works. Zoos have found clicker training a stress-free way to move their giraffes from one pen to another, or to urge a Himalayan bear to stand on his hind legs so they can check the underbelly through a gridded door for any possible problems. A clicker sound is a constant. Training depends on consistency. It is hard enough for a rabbit to figure out what a human wants when he has to decode a strange language, your motions, or what your touch is trying to convey.

You will need to buy a clicker, or find an adequate substitute. I used a binder clip to make a "snap" sound until I found it was a lot more work for my fingers than using a clicker. Clickers cost between $4 and $8, and I bought mine at a pet store. I saw clickers in the pet department of a discount store.

You'll need to lay in at least a couple of different treats, to keep boredom from setting in. The treats don't have to be sweet; if your bunny gets little pelleted food as part of his regular diet, he might go gaga when treated with a pellet as a reward. The same is true of tiny carrot sticks or carrot cubes. (Some rabbit keepers try to use the sweet things like blueberries or raisins only once in a while or to reward success for a difficult trick.) I've seen rabbits perfectly happy to be rewarded with a small piece of collard greens.

The big point in clicker training is seeing the "Aha" moment, when your rabbit puts two and two together and realizes he can cause

Clicker training is a fast way to teach desired actions.

the clicker to sound and thus he gets a reward. Eventually you can decrease the treats and use the clicker coupled with a quick petting, but at first the click and the food reward are the motivating forces.

Plan on spending anywhere from 10 minutes to half an hour on each training session, depending on your rabbit's level of interest. Try to keep the training fun and tedium-free. Daily is good; every other day is almost as good. Repetition is the key. Once you begin working with your rabbit, you'll find the training makes the time go quite quickly, and the net result, a well-socialized bunny trained to obey simple commands, is well worth it.

Starting is simple. Sit down with your rabbit, click, and give him a treat. If he is too shy to take the food from your hand, put it on the ground. Let him eat his reward (keep the pieces small). Wait a few minutes and repeat. If he wants to hop around, let him. Give him a few minutes, click, and give a treat. The object is for your bunny to associate the noise of the clicker with you and something fun and enjoyable.

Once you can see that he looks for a treat at the sound of a click, go to the next step, which is reinforcing movement. Let's use teaching "Come" as your first command; that is certainly a useful behavior. Move back a step or so from your bunny, show him the treat, and say "Come." Wait until he moves toward you, click, and reward. Move back, and repeat. Let him hop away from you, give the "Come" command, and when he makes a move toward you, click and treat. Click and treat when he moves toward you again. Soon he'll associate the word "Come" with moving toward you, a click, and a treat. Don't hesitate to show affection when he behaves as you wish.

If your rabbit's cage sits directly on the floor, you can teach him to go back into his cage on command using a clicker. Pick him up, place him in front of his open cage, and tell him "Go home." Toss a treat into the cage in front of him and click as he hops in. You can work on the "Come" command when he finishes the treat and turns around to face the entrance of the cage (turning around to face the entrance of a cage is a pretty dependable, normal rabbit behavior). Once he hops out and has his reward, this gives you a chance to back up and work on the "Come" command two or three times more.

Jumping. Select the object you want your bunny to jump over, and put it on the ground between you and your bunny. The jumping barrier can be a section of PVC pipe or a long low box. Start with the barrier laid flat on the ground. Put your bunny on the far side of the jump and give him the "Come" command. As he jumps over the barrier to get to you, give the command "Jump," and click. Reward with a treat when your bunny comes up to you. Move and replace the barrier and repeat the "Come" command. Follow with the "Jump" command when your rabbit hops over the barricade. Give him the treat; he's earned it!

Conversely, if you have a helper, you can place your rabbit in front of the low obstacle and use your hands to urge him over it with the "Jump" command. Your helper's role is to click as the jump takes place and then to issue the reward.

Once your bunny hops over the barricade at the "Jump" command, you can increase the height or the width incrementally. The important aspect of creating a jump "obstacle" is that the barrier must be lightweight and must fall down if the rabbit bumps into it; you don't want him to crash into something immobile. It's important that your rabbit isn't frightened or injured when he misjudges a jump. Remember to praise him for his actions, and to make the training process a positive process.

If you want to teach your rabbit to jump through a hoop, make certain it is large enough so he can jump through it without feeling cramped for space. You may

The click reinforces desired actions, like going through a tunnel.

Using a training mat

Some rabbit owners find a training mat helps get the message across to the rabbit something fun is going to take place. A training mat is just a folded towel or a small mat you use only when training, something that gives your rabbit good footing. You pick up the mat and put it away at the end of every session. You can also use another mat, just inside the rabbit's cage door. Your rabbit will quickly learn to sit on her mat when she wants you to take her out of cage so she can play. Provide several treats at the end of each session so the rabbit's fun can go on a bit longer.

Your rabbit will very soon understand the mat means training, fun, and rewards. When you call your rabbit, pat the mat so the rabbit will stand on it when she completes the command. Put her on the mat when you train her to turn in circles or to push the ball. When you want to train her to sit on your lap, put the mat across your stretched-out legs while you're sitting on the floor. Tell your rabbit to come, and pat the mat on top of your legs. Your rabbit will be nervous about jumping onto a nonflat surface, but after several sessions she'll understand the command and the treat.

Use this same technique if you want your rabbit to sit next to you on the sofa. Put the mat on the floor next to the sofa, and tell her "Come." When she responds, click and give her a treat. After she does this a few times, pick the mat up and put it on the sofa next to you, but pull it forward so it flops over the front edge of the sofa. Give a "Sofa up" command. Click when your rabbit responds correctly, and give her a treat.

Once your rabbit understands she has to stand on her hind legs in order to get her reward, pull the mat back so it is next to you on the sofa, and work on the "Sofa up" command. Soon she will understand she needs to hop up onto the mat on the sofa next to you in order to get the click.

wish to set the hoop vertically within a Styrofoam block "brace," or you can enlist a helper to hold the hoop very steady as your rabbit jumps through. Give your rabbit the "Jump" command and click as he hops through the hoop. Incrementally increase the height of the hoop as your rabbit becomes more skilled.

Touching an object. When your bunny is in front of you, ready for another treat, put a small ball down near her. This can be a plastic ball with a bell inside, a ball you make by putting the ring-sections cut from a paper towel roll inside each other, or even a small plastic kiddie car. Put the treat on top of the object and give your bunny the "Touch" command. Your bunny will touch the object in picking up the treat. Click as she touches the object. Pick up the ball. Put the ball down again, near the bunny, and repeat the "Touch" command. After two or three successful touches, stop placing the treat on top of the object but reward with a treat after the action has been completed. Decrease the treat rewards, and let the click and your affection be the reward.

When she has the Touch aspect mastered, you can move onto Push. Create a slight incline, by placing the object on top of a thin book with a pencil under one end, or put the object at the very edge of a mouse pad, so the slightest touch would push it over the edge. Give the "Touch" command, but as he reaches to nose the object, change the command to "Push." Click when the object moves. Reward your bunny.

As your rabbit begins to understand the idea behind Push, set a goal for her to aim toward—perhaps just a colored square on the ground. Clicking does require work on the part of your rabbit—she has to figure out what you're talking about *this* time, so try to make it easy for her to act.

If your rabbit begins to miss the point of any increase in the training, go back a step and make certain

The rabbit soon learns that a "click" means he's done the right thing. At first each action needs to be rewarded with a bit of a treat.

you're rewarding good actions and just ignoring the bad. Lavish praise on your rabbit for her skills in any aspect of training, and keep the lessons varied.

As you can see, clicker training strengthens the bond between you

The Touch command is the basis for more complicated commands.

You can clicker train your rabbit to go back into his cage upon "Go Home."

and your rabbit, and the development of that bond is one of the big reasons why you have a rabbit. Your rabbit actually works to find ways to elicit the clicker response from you. In effect, deciding who is training who becomes a little sticky.

Clicking and distracting

You can use a clicker to divert your rabbit from doing something undesirable. You're actually distracting him, offering a substitute behavior, and then clicking. For instance, if your rabbit's cage is actually a rabbit pen made from grid squares, your rabbit may have developed the habit of moving his cage by physically seizing grid sections in his teeth and shoving them outward, or pulling them in. To extinguish an undesired behavior like this, give your rabbit the "No

Nugget's first clicker training was to jump onto a low box.

shake" command. When he pauses and gives you the "Oh, yeah?" look to see if you're taking this in, tell him "No shake" again, click, and treat. You're working here to reward him when he isn't grabbing the cage grids.

It would also help if you offered more play items, items he can easily take in his mouth and toss around as substitutes for pen moving. Give him something to do. The more time he spends tossing around a soft cube, or one of those tiny handleless cups you can buy in the baby section of your grocery store, the less time he will have to move his cage. Rabbits are smart, and yours may have figured a sure way to get a treat would be to grab the cage grid and shove it around.

This same technique works with biters. Rabbits bite when they are frustrated with how they are treated despite giving earlier signals they may have given earlier (see Chapter 5 on talking rabbit). Work around the biting issue by leaving the rabbit in his cage for the first few sessions. When he responds to your presence and your offer of a treat by coming to the front of the cage, click and treat. Repeat this click-means-no-handling-and-a-treat training until the rabbit comes to the front of the cage readily when he sees you approach. Open the cage door and use the clicker to train him to accept a tickle between the eyes and around the ears. Open the cage door and continue the training on social grooming. You may need to backslide the click-and-treat association until your bunny no longer fears your hands and nudges you for more petting.

Ears flying, Spyro the Mini-Lop clears the rail. Many hopping rabbits are clicker trained.

Chapter Eight

Hopping and Agility

Rabbit jumping (called rabbit hopping) and rabbit agility are two new ways to exercise and train your rabbit. These activities can be done at home with just you and your rabbits, or they can be done on a competitive basis.

Agility and hopping are especially suited to outgoing rabbits that like to spend time out of their cage (but keep in mind that TLC and "going places" will help make any rabbit more outgoing).

All kinds of rabbits can enjoy hopping and agility. You may hear that there are some breeds that are physically inept at jumping or agility. The list of not-supposed-to-be-great-jumpers-or-agility-rabbits includes the rabbits bred for meat, like the New Zealand White; those with long ears, like the English Lops; the tiny dwarf types; and those with long or wooly fur. There are some solid reasons why some breeds would be less than able jumpers.

The meat rabbits are bred for their weight, and as the Iowa Hopping Club admits, it's like asking a Clydesdale horse to jump. Long-eared types are hampered by the length and weight of their ears. The dwarf breeds, like the Netherlands dwarf, have little bones along with their tiny stature, and they just aren't great jumpers. Angora and Jersey Woolys have a lot of fur, and their fur may restrict their vision. Short-bodied Dutch rabbits may not have the body length needed to make it over jumps that require a reach. If you have one of these purebred rabbits, you may want to tone down your training sessions and simply enter competitions if you and your rabbit will enjoy them. There's nothing wrong with something done just for the fun of it.

Rabbit hopping

Rabbit jumping or rabbit hopping is a rabbit sport that features rabbits' native ability to jump. Hopping is modeled directly from horse steeplechase events, scaled down for rabbits. Like steeplechase, hopping events are timed events. Ratings are given for speed and how well the rabbit negotiates the

A lop clears a high jump.

jumps. A "clean go" means the course was completed with no errors or faults.

Jumps may or may not be arranged around the perimeter of a square; the square setup is used where space is very limited. When space permits, the jump course may be along a more complex pathway. There may even be several jump courses in a single event.

The jumps are wide or high or a combination, and there is usually a water hazard. As with steeplechase for horses, the obstacles are designed to fall apart when touched, so a rabbit who fails to clear a jump won't be injured. Rabbits know the jumps aren't solid, and you may occasionally see a competing rabbit pause before a jump, reach up and delicately shove the top bar so it falls down. Then the rabbit completes the jump. Audiences love these little idiosyncrasies.

In rabbit hopping, the rabbit may or may not be on a leash during its "go" (a "go" is the rabbit's effort to complete the course). Some rabbit-jumping groups forego the leash requirement when the event is staged in an enclosed indoor ring. They feel the leash takes away from the spontaneity of the event; if a rabbit won't jump for the joy of jumping without the tether of a leash, the exercise is pointless. Although treats are a good way to encourage behavior during training, treat awards are not allowed in the ring. It is important that you help your rabbit enjoy hopping just for the fun of it.

Although they have compact bodies and short legs, Dutch and lops can be trained in jumping and agility.

Rabbit jumping developed in Sweden in the late 1970s as rabbit keepers there looked for a more interactive and hands-on way to work with their bunnies. The Swedish Federation of Rabbit Jumping was formed in 1994, and that organization set up standards for jumping and criteria for judge selection. Other jumping organizations have been set up in Norway, Finland, Denmark, and England. English "jumping" began after a rabbit enthusiast brought the sport back to England; their first hopping exhibition was in 2009.

Rabbit jumping in these early-start countries has progressed to a level of sophistication we don't have in the United States. In Sweden, a competition has four events, each with four levels of difficulty. The events are the straight track, the winding track, the long jump,

and the high jump. Tracks have between 8 and 12 obstacles, and the rabbit is supposed to negotiate each track in a set order with minimal urging from its owner. When a rabbit has gained three points at the same level, it has qualified to compete at the next higher level, until it has reached the elite level. There are two groupings for the long and high jump: "non-elite" followed by "elite." Rabbits that compete successfully at the non-elite level advance to the elite level, and those who compete successfully at the elite level gain a certificate. Three certificates and the rabbit adds "Champion" to his or her name, as in Champion Fifi.

Rabbit hopping in the United States until very recently has been of limited interest; it was usually limited to 4-H participants training their rabbits and setting up an exhibition as a project. In 2011, an exhibition of rabbit hopping by the Iowa Hopping Group at the national ARBA Convention put national focus on this sport for the first time. National groups have formed: the American Association of Sporting Events for Rabbits (rabbit sports in general), the Iowa Hopping Group (hopping), and the Rabbit Hopping Organization of America (agility and hopping).

The Iowa Hopping Group created their own guidelines and adopted jump standards and construction tips from those furnished by the Swedish and other hopping clubs. The guidelines are still evolving; if hopping becomes an ARBA-sanctioned event, there is the question yet to be answered about following ARBA's show standards. These standards include requiring ear tattoos for entered rabbits and favoring purebred species over rabbit "mutts."

The newness of rabbit hopping means there currently are no international standards; the South Australia Rabbit Fanciers Society, for instance, puts its jump bars no higher than 11 inches (28 cm). The record high jump for the Swedish hopping group is 39 inches (99 cm).

Although the Iowa Hopping Group's standards for competition are not national standards, these guidelines might be a logical place to start if you are interested in rabbit hopping. If there is no rabbit hopping group in your area, you may want to start one. Because this interest is such a new approach to rabbit appreciation, the field is wide open for anyone or any group to run a local event. All it takes is a small group of dedicated volunteers who can select a date (alignment with a local or state fair would be very helpful in terms of creating interest and in promoting the event), acquire the use of a facility, plan the promotion, design the course, and then recruit judges and contestants.

Beginning training for jumping

Your rabbit needs to be in her harness, partly so she'll know she is about to have fun (and also so that you can leash her when she isn't competing, when that time comes).

Set up your first jumps. They don't have to be anything formal so it won't take much time. Your first jumps might be a long low box and a 3-foot (91 cm) length of PVC pipe, with at least a one-hop space (6 feet) between them.

Place your bunny at the first jump. Watch her for a moment; some bunnies will leap over anything at any time without any direction. You may find you'll need to guide her with your hands below and behind her, and to tell her "Jump!"

When she jumps the first barricade, whether on her own or after a bit of urging, tell her "Good Bunny!" and urge her over the second. When she completes the second jump, pet her, give her a treat, tell her what a great bunny she is, and repeat the process.

You'll need to repeat the exercise at intervals until it begins to stick; many rabbit trainers use just 10 minutes on a trick before they train for a new one.

Remember to praise and reward positive actions and to ignore the actions you don't want. Let your rabbit tell you when she's getting tired of being trained. Pick up the training again that afternoon or the next day.

When you're ready to train for a higher jump, place the PVC pipe across two towers you create. Your first towers might be books that will lift the pole 2 inches or so off the ground. Keep the PVC on top of the

A smart rabbit takes down the bars so he can go **through** *the jump—it's easier that way.*

book(s) so it will roll off harmlessly if your bunny hits it. You can build towers, using two 6-inch square pieces of plywood as feet for two 24-inch (61 cm) lengths of 2 × 2s. Place pairs of fencing staples in a v-pattern along one side of each 2 × 2 at 2-inch (5 cm) intervals to provide support for the PVC cross bars. The "V" placement helps hold the crossbar in place, but the crossbar is easily knocked down.

Books, laid on their sides, work well for broad jumping. Your rabbit may see the jump and jump over it with no urging from you. You may need to direct her over the jump, using your hands and your voice. In any case, praise her and reward her for making the jump.

You can create a water course from a 12 × 15-inch (30 × 30 cm) baking pan, placed at first upside down, so your rabbit jumps over the flat surface of the bottom. Your rabbit will jump over the shorter dimension. Make certain your rabbit can clear a jump of this width before you turn the dish over and add water; landing in water unexpectedly may frighten your rabbit.

Taking jumping to a higher level

When you are ready to join a jumping group, or if you decide to train for an exhibition, you'll need more standardized jumps. You can buy commercially made dog jumps

A-frames may be used in jumping or agility courses.

and modify them, or you can make the jumps. Jumps are made of PVC pipes or wood or a combination of the two. The jump bases are usually painted white, and the horizontal bars are painted a bright color or striped with brightly colored electrician's tape to make them easier for a rabbit to see. The crossbar should be able to be moved up at 4-inch (10 cm) intervals.

Agility

Rabbit agility is modeled upon dog agility, but with scaled-down jumps and exercises.

The obstacles vary from on-ground obstacles like tunnels, chutes, weave poles, seesaws, tables, A-frames, and rabbitwalks (the rabbit walks along a raised plank) to high jumps, hoop jumps, and broad jumps. Like rabbit hopping, the goal in rabbit agility is to complete the course with few errors (called faults) as quickly as possible.

The rabbit may or may not be off leash, depending on the course and the sponsor's rules. The handler runs alongside the rabbit, either holding the leash or directing the rabbit with directions and body language. If the course requires a leash, the handler must not use the leash to direct the rabbit; the leash must be loose at all times.

Rabbits get quite good at agility; it simply gives them a way to hone the skills that would keep a wild rabbit alive. (When you actually get to watch a competition, you'll see the ones who are trying not to stumble over their own feet tend to be the rabbit owners.)

Due to space limitations and ease of setup, agility courses are usually set up in a square with the owner/handler running alongside the rabbit. This sort of setup works well whether the rabbit is leashed

Jasper the Dutch rabbit sails over a jump at the Honley agricultural show in West Yorkshire, England.

help design these courses (Clean Course Designer is one example). Rabbits that have been trained/have experience in navigating different types of jumps are generally unafraid of a new course.

Beginning training for agility

You will need to put your pet in his harness before you begin training, so he'll know something good is going to happen. You won't need a leash in these early exercises, because you'll need both hands to help direct your bunny.

Put your rabbit down in front of his first obstacle. If you want to start with jumps, set up vertical and broad jumps for his first training sessions. The advantage of starting with jumping for agility training is that jumping is natural behavior for rabbits.

Once your rabbit has mastered the basics of jumping, set up a set of weave poles in your backyard or training area. You can use 36-inch-long (91 cm) bamboo poles or 36-inch (91 cm) lengths of 1-inch (3 cm) PVC pipes, stuck into the ground, or you can go to a farm supply store and buy a half dozen 48-inch (122 cm) UV-resistant polyolefin step-in posts. (These posts run about $3 each; they are designed to hold electrical wires for a "hot" fence, but they work very well for weave poles.)

or unleashed. Other courses, where the rabbit is not leashed, have a more creative design, with the course often crossing over itself. There is even computer software to

Sometimes a rabbit refuses to jump, and that's OK.

How to Set Up an Agility Course

Here's a basic course guideline set up by Dawn Nelsey of A Basket of Blessings Rabbitry of Hale, Michigan. She melded guidelines from the Canadian Rabbit Hopping Club, 4-H rules, and a book called *Rabbit Agility: What's That?* By Dell Robbins.

Agility classes
Novice: Easy course
- This class is for all first- and second-time agility competition rabbits.
- Obstacles may be placed in a straight line or a simple U-shaped course. Obstacles must 6′ apart.
- There will be 6 to 12 obstacles: Novice A Maximum 4″ (10 cm) jumps, two rails wide for spread jumps; Novice B Maximum 8″ (20 cm) jumps, two rails wide for spread jumps.

The following obstacles are used:
Pipe tunnel
A-Frame
Spread jumps
Vertical jumps
Pause box and/or table

Intermediate: Medium course
- This class is for rabbits who have completed the Novice class.
- Obstacles may be placed in a straight line or a simple M or U shaped course. Obstacles must be 6′6″ apart.
- There will be 8 to 14 obstacles: Jumps Maximum of 12″ (30 cm) high, three rails wide for spread jumps

The following obstacles are used:
Pipe tunnel
A-frame
Spread jumps

The poles should be placed about a foot apart. Place your rabbit at one end and offer a treat at the side of the first pole. As your rabbit moves to take the treat, move it to the outside of the next pole. When he moves to take it, move to the outside of the next pole. Weave him through four poles and give him his treat and praise him. He'll learn what to do with weave poles pretty quickly.

Rabbits are nervous creatures and rarely stay in one place for long. The pause box, a marked square on the ground, should also be part of your training (the pause table is a raised platform of perhaps 4 inches that your rabbit must hop onto and stay motionless for the count of five). Place the box or mark a square on the ground in your training area. Place your rabbit on the box or in the square and tell him "Stay." Hold him for the count of five. Release him, tell him he is a good rabbit, and then reward him. Repeat four or five times and move on to another task.

The chute is an open tunnel (or bottomless bucket) with a fabric tube on one end. The other end of the fabric tube lacks any sort of support so it lies flat on the ground. Place your rabbit at the open end of the tunnel, urge him to enter, and

A harness and leash may not be required in some competitions.

tell him "Chute." Once he experiences that the fabric tube at the end simply closes around him like a tunnel and the end is open, his reluctance to enter will end.

A good way to teach your rabbit how to negotiate the A-frame is to start him near the top. Lead him to the top and down the other side with a treat. Once he understands his job is to reach the top of the A-frame and to run down the other side, you can start him a little further down the upward side of the frame. Be patient with him until he gets the hang of going up and going down.

Once your rabbit understands two agility challenges, have him go through both of them, one right after the other, before you reward him. When he's able to do two tasks, add another task he has already learned. Be lavish with your praise and perhaps a treat or two at the end.

Use gentle urging, praise, and repetition to teach your rabbit how to negotiate all of the agility obstacles you have. You will soon be able to tell if your rabbit enjoys agility. Some rabbits, despite the positive reinforcement of praise, treat, and the activity of training, may never show much enthusiasm for the process. Others may even do a binky when they're leaping over a jump, letting you know that they're having fun.

Agility gives your rabbit the opportunity to evaluate new challenges, both horizontally and verti-

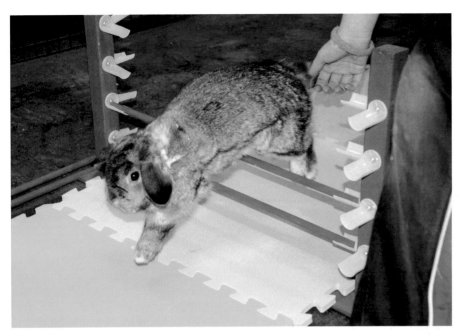

"I get by with a little nudge from my friends." Handlers are permitted to urge their rabbit to jump but can only use their hands.

cally. The choices you can offer are limited only by the space you have to work in and how much you want to spend. You can buy a set of basic dog agility equipment (weave poles, open tunnel, high jump, and a pause box) for about $50, or you can make what you need.

Making your own agility props

Vertical jumps. A length of PVC pipe, a yard stick, or broom handle across two stacks of books.

Bunny Walk or Bridge. A 24-inch (61 cm) length of 1 × 12 board, with 12 × 18-inch (30 ×

46 cm) ramps at each end, held in place by screwed-in angle irons, bent open to a 60-degree angle.

Broad jumps. For a broad jump, stack 36-inch long (91 cm) lengths of scrap wood in groups, 3 to 4 inches (8 to 10 cm) apart.

Tunnel. Use a collapsible fabric laundry basket, the kind that opens into a netted tube when you put laundry in it. Remove the bottom so you have a 24-inch (61 cm) mesh tube when it is extended. The laundry basket tunnel works for small rabbits. For larger rabbits, use a kid's play tunnel, a dog agility tunnel, or a large cardboard tunnel (the 12-inch (30 cm) concrete casting tubes work well, and can be pur-

Rabbits soon have no fear of new agility obstacles like the tunnel.

chased in 4-foot (122 cm) lengths at larger home improvement stores).

Chute. A plastic garbage can or 5-gallon paint bucket with the bottom sawed out (a hacksaw works well if you don't have a circular saw) and a sheet sewn into a tube to fit over the far end makes a workable chute.

A-frame. Use two wooden planks or plywood 12 to 18 inches (30 to 46 cm) wide, hinged at the junction to form an "A" shape and braced with hooks and eyes so the peak is about 18 inches (46 cm) off the ground. Use carpeting or narrow cross strips nailed in place to provide safe footing.

Jump circles. Create a jump circle with a hula hoop or half-inch aquarium tubing bent into a circle and taped together.

Water jump. A broom handle resting atop a large metal baking dish or kitty litter pan, with an inch or so of water inside, function as a water jump.

Teeter totter. A 3- to 4-foot (91 to 122 cm) plank, 8 to 12 inches (20 to 30 cm) wide, covered with fabric to provide more secure footing, placed over the "totter" cylinder. I used a foot long piece of PVC pipe for the totter, and added 4 × 4-inch braces on each end, secured to each other by drilling two holes near the center of each brace. I pulled the braces and the PVC together using a wire run through the holes with the PVC in the center.

Pause table. Wrap fabric around a stack of books 2′ × 2′ × 6″ (5 × 5 × 15 cm) high.

Weave poles. Cut 1-inch (2.5 cm) PVC pipes or wooden dowels into 24-inch (61 cm) lengths and stick them into the ground a foot apart. The step-in post on page 66 might be easier to set up and take down.

Chapter Nine
Your Rabbit's Health

Your rabbit-in-training may never have a moment's worth of illness. The advances made in husbandry techniques and medical care in the past 25 years have made keeping a pet rabbit healthy a very uncomplicated process. Yet sometimes things do go wrong, and if you can see what's happening early on, it's easier/faster/cheaper to correct things. You are your rabbit's first line of defense when it comes to his health.

The rabbit's exterior

Mites. Your pet rabbit ought not have any problems with mites, but in the event that you acquire a rabbit from a doubtful source (one of my friends found hers in a box at a bus stop!), you'll need to know what to look out for.

Ear mites are blood sucking, eight-legged tick relatives, just smaller than the period at the end of this sentence. Under a microscope, they look like a squatty arm-waving Michelin Man with the head truncated down to a mouth (I apologize for this mental image but it's pretty close). Mites hook themselves into a place inside the rabbit's ear, or many other convenient places, and pierce the skin with their sucking mouth parts to begin feeding. They take frequent breaks

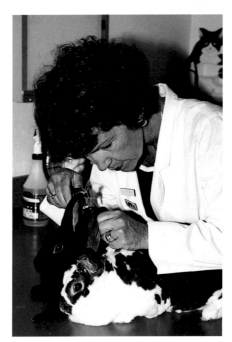

A veterinarian checks a pair of Rex rabbits for ear mites.

Good nutrition will prevent most illnesses.

Mites make rabbits itch. Rabbits with ear mites will hold their head tilted over to one side, shaking the head, as if to dislodge something in the ear. They will scratch or rub their heads/ears against the side of the cage or on furniture. Rabbit's big ears give mites plenty of room to settle in, and they can make your rabbit very uncomfortable.

You can do a quick check for mites by looking into your rabbit's ears. Look for extreme dandruff, crusty-looking areas, and brownish-black deposits. You may encounter some mild resistance on the part of your rabbit to having her ears examined; those ears are now very tender (yours would be too, I can assure you). Your veterinarian will diagnose mites by taking a swabbing from inside the ear or a scraping from the skin and looking at the scraping under a microscope.

Ivermectin is the gold standard to get rid of mites. It is a very safe, inexpensive, and effective injectable drug used against all external parasites. It begins working its magic within 24 hours. The regimen needs to be repeated in three weeks, to eliminate mites that have hatched since the first injection. You won't need to bathe your rabbit or do anything special other than very thoroughly cleaning the cage area weekly and making sure your rabbit goes for her second treatment. A topical treatment called selamectin is also available.

You can treat for mites yourself (it takes far longer than if you

to find another mite of the opposite sex and to reproduce prodigiously.

Rabbits pick up mites through contact with an infested rabbit, through dirty caging, or by lying on nesting material that contains the mites or their eggs. Contact with contaminated rabbit droppings is a common mode of transmission. Rabbits that have been poorly housed are an open buffet for mites.

involve your veterinarian), or you can use this remedy if you discover the problem on a Friday night and can't get to your veterinarian until Monday.

Use an eyedropper to put a half teaspoon or so of mineral oil or baby oil into your rabbit's ears. Mineral oil coats the mite's body and plugs up his little spiracles which means the mites just suffocate. Repeat this treatment twice a week for three weeks. Using mineral oil is a pre-miracle-drug-era procedure, one that was highly in favor in the dark ages of rabbit husbandry of the 1950s, but it does work. It's just a lot slower than the medication your veterinarian can prescribe. Your rabbit will not receive the 24-hour relief she will with Ivermectin, but she will feel better within a week.

Sore hocks. Also known as ulcerative pododermatitis, sore hocks are a common problem in pet rabbits kept in dirty cages with little opportunity to move around. The rabbit develops ulcers or open sores on the lower side of his ankles, and the ulcers can't heal because they are placed against unyielding wire mesh or against piled-up rabbit urine and droppings (they are pretty much the equivalent of bed sores in humans). The ulcer begins with a small foot sore that becomes secondarily infected. The problem is further complicated if the rabbit is kept in a damp cage, a cage too small to permit much freedom of movement, or a cage has a

Heavy dandruff in the ears may indicate mites.

wire bottom cage with no smooth place to rest. This malady may also arise if a rabbit is allowed to get so fat it places extra pressure on the bottoms of the feet.

Treatment consists of alleviating the cage conditions that caused the problem, cleaning the sores with antiseptic solution or with soap and water and rinsing well, and then putting antibiotic ointment on the sores. You may need a prescription for an oral antibiotic (liquids are easier to administer; pills must be crushed and administered, mixed with fruit jam or in a liquid or semiliquid form). Rabbits usually will remove any sort of bandage you place around or on their feet, so you'll need to avoid any sort of moisture on the feet by keeping the caging dry.

Since this sort of infection seriously damages the foot tissues, the problem won't go away in just a few days. Stick with the treatment until the foot sores heal. Any sort of training must be halted until healing is completed.

Bacterial skin infections. Rabbits, especially the larger rabbits with a pronounced dewlap, offered water from a watering dish tend to wet their dewlap when they stick their heads in the water to drink. The moist dewlap folds are a ready-made environment for *Pseudomonas* bacteria, which produces a distinct bad odor and is very uncomfortable for your rabbit. Clip the hair from the chin area. Dry it as best as you can, and put on an antibiotic cream or powder a couple of times daily (you can buy triple antibiotic creams and powders at your drugstore). The area must be kept dry. Change the watering system to a water bottle hung on the outside of the cage, or add a large rubber ball to the water crock so your rabbit can't get his head far enough in to wet the dewlap. Make sure the ball is pet safe; a ball that is not pet safe may leech plastic into the water, hardly what you want to happen.

You can also elevate the water crock a few inches so your rabbit can't stick his head in the water as far, but make sure he can still get all the water he needs.

Dental problems

Rabbits, despite your best efforts, can run into things. They can careen into a bookcase when running around the house; they can run into other objects when they misjudge distances. Competitive jumps are constructed to where they fall down easily, without much impact from your rabbit, but accidents can happen almost anywhere. Suddenly you realize your rabbit has a broken tooth, one of the big ones in front.

Although you're upset about the tooth (as is your rabbit) check over the entire rabbit as part of the initial treatment assay. Rabbits have thin bones and not much protection in the thoracic area. The broken tooth may require pain relief (this means a visit to your local veterinarian). The incisors must be examined, usually under a light anesthetic. If the pulp of the tooth is exposed, your veterinarian will remove the pulp in the distal part of the tooth, and then fill in the canal with calcium hydroxide cement. As the cement hardens, it will protect the pulp from any further exposure to air.

Now all that needs to be done is to monitor the opposite tooth, and to trim it, to compensate for the lack of wear. If there's no damage to the tooth base of the damaged tooth, the rabbit's fast-growing teeth will "even up" with time. If the damaged tooth does not grow, your choice is to have the opposing teeth removed, or keep up with the tooth trimming.

Rabbits' teeth grow all the time, on the average about 1 to 2 mm a month. The teeth wear against each other, which keeps them all at the right length. For a normal rabbit, the paired incisors and cheek teeth do not occlude at the same time. When molars and premolars are used to chew food, incisors are separated. When the incisors are used, the molars do not touch. When a rabbit pulls a tuft of hay into its mouth and begins to chew it with its molars, you can see the jaw actually shift position, to bring the back teeth against each other. If either the incisors or molars/premolars don't match up, your rabbit cannot cut or chew its food effectively, leading to reduced food intake and poor health.

Of all the breeds, the dwarf breeds tend to be the ones with maloccluded teeth because their jaw projects forward when at rest. This causes incisors to wear abnormally. Inspect your rabbit's mouth and check the teeth about once a month. Just lift him up, cradle him on his back, and use your fingers to gently part his lips to check the front teeth, and then move his lips slightly to check the molars on each side. What you're looking for is abnormal wear patterns, the lack of wear, or ridges. It can be difficult to see the teeth in the back of the mouth; this may be something you add to the checklist you'll use for a veterinarian visit. Your veterinarian may use an otoscope or endoscope to check the back teeth. Sedation or anesthesia may be required to visualize them fully, and your veterinarian won't take this risk unless it

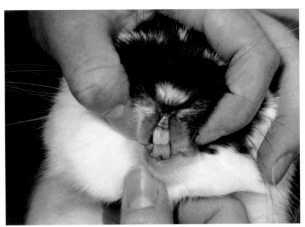

Checking your rabbit's front teeth for possible damage.

is clearly indicated. Incisor malocclusions, lack of appetite, excessive salivation, and drooling can all indicate a problem with the molar teeth and call for action on your part.

Once in a while, when there is congenital incisor malocclusion, it may be necessary to remove the incisors. Rabbits have prehensile lips and tongues so they'll still be able to feed themselves, although some precut food must be added to the diet to ensure adequate fiber intake.

Horizontal ridges in teeth indicate a problem in calcium levels–your rabbit isn't getting enough. All animals need a specific level of calcium in their blood. If calcium levels are low, the body takes calcium from the teeth and bones to maintain the blood levels. This is hazardous for a rabbit involved in training, especially agility or jumping.

Once the rabbit's diet is modified to include additional calcium, the ridges will grow out. It's important to correct this because demineralized teeth (teeth lacking calcium and other minerals) are accompanied by calcium loss in the supporting jaw and in other bones. In the jaw, abscesses tend to form in the most demineralized areas as the teeth roots elongate and penetrate the jawbone. The unsupported teeth tend to move, and the elongated roots can be felt along the lower edge of the lower jaw as lumps. The abscesses can form in the tooth root area, which is difficult to cure with simple lancing and flushing. Abscesses that form in the roof of the mouth can infect the nasal cavity and grow under the globe of the eye. You can see why simply checking your rabbit's teeth can matter.

The rabbit's interior

The best known and often least understood health problem for domestic rabbits is called "snuffles." The term refers to a chronic upper respiratory infection, usually due to a *Pasturella* bacteria (less frequently, *Bordetella*, the same bacteria that causes kennel cough in dogs). When caused by the *Pasteurella* bacteria, the infection is called pasteurellosis. The first symptom is a runny nose, but the discharge becomes thicker and discolored. If your rabbit begins to breathe through her mouth, she's in serious trouble. She is unlikely to get better on her own.

Pasteurellosis is easily transmitted to other rabbits by direct contact or through infected objects. It primarily enters the body through the nasal passages, although it travels throughout the body. Rabbits may display no sign of infection but be carriers nonetheless. Poor ventilation and the concomitant high levels of ammonia seem to contribute to the incidence of the disease.

For many rabbits, the only sign of infection is rhinitis or a runny nose. Invisible but part of the complex are toxins given off by some bacterial strains, erosion of the rabbit's inner nose, inflammation of the lungs (pleurisy), inflammation of the heart, abscesses, and ear infection. Pasteurellosis is not a harmless malady.

Treatment usually begins with a sensitivity test to determine which antibiotics the bacterium is sensitive to, or a broad spectrum antibiotic like Baytril may be prescribed. Antibiotic therapy may eliminate the bacteria, but in many cases antibiotics will only control it. Other therapies, such as eye drops, may be needed to control the spread of the disease. Keeping the environment clean also helps prevent the spread.

Viral hemorrhagic disease (VHD), or rabbit calci virus, is a viral disease of rabbits that is highly contagious and usually fatal. Outbreaks are so rapidly dealt with (any rabbitry with this infection has all rabbits euthanized) that the disease to date has been contained and eliminated.

The virus reproduces in the liver and damages the liver. The damaged liver cells release thromboplastins, which in turn initiate hemorrhages in the lungs and kidneys. The highly infectious disease is very painful to rabbits. Upon dissection, gross signs of the disease are limited to a few hemorrhages in large muscles. VHD first appeared in China in 1984, and spread to Europe, Asia, Africa, and North America. A field test in Australia in 1995 was confined to an island, but the virus "escaped" to the Australian mainland within 6 months. The spread of this disease—which is restricted to rabbits—did help control the wild rabbit population in that country.

In the United States, two of our native species, the Black-tailed Jackrabbits and the Eastern Cottontails are resistant to the virus. But the European rabbit (and hence all domestic rabbits) is fully susceptible. The implications for every aspect of the domestic rabbit industry are vast, which is why any confirmed cases must be reported to your state veterinarian as well as the Animal and Plant Health Inspection Service, a branch of the U.S. Department of Agriculture.

Abscesses. Rabbits may develop abscesses almost anywhere on their bodies, but abscesses usually appear on the head or legs. The causative agent is generally *Pasteurella* or a *Staphylococcus* bacteria. For no apparent reason, swellings appear on the rabbit's head or legs over the period of a week or so. The swellings are not painful, but once these bacteria are entrenched, they can be very difficult to eliminate. The abscess tends to involve any underlying bone, which serves as a reservoir for the bacteria. Abscesses on the jaw can be a very real problem because there's not much bone that can be removed to dispose of the infection.

The treatment may include surgical removal of the infected flesh and bone, along with antibiotic therapy; sensitivity tests will indicate the best antibiotic to use. Sometimes the infection of the bone is so advanced that the only choice is euthanization. Gainesville Rabbit Rescue had a rescue named Nova whose "sore hocks" and advanced malnutrition meant weeks of one-on-one home care by a veterinary technician, before surgery to remove infected flesh and bone could be attempted. It was then discovered the infection had spread to her pelvic girdle. There is a limit to what TLC and medical care can do.

Spaying or neutering

Spaying or neutering your rabbit can be the best thing you can do to

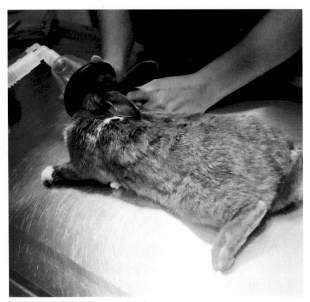

Administering gas anesthesia.

spraying urine, the changing hormone levels result in more aggression, mounting behavior, and dislike of being handled (including scratching with his claws). Is this any way to live?

Unspayed females also spray their urine and become aggressive. Spaying of course prevents pregnancy, a good enough reason on its own. But spaying also is used to prevent uterine cancer. The incidence of uterine cancer in unsprayed does approaches 80% by the age of 4.

Cost for spay/neuter varies depending on where you live, but the surgery for a female or doe is more expensive than for the male or buck. Call around because it can make a real difference, and if your humane society offers a low-cost certificate, buy it. Make sure you take your pet to an experienced rabbit veterinarian for the surgery. A low-cost procedure is not such a good deal if the rabbit doesn't recover from surgery.

Surgery

Postsurgical Tips

About sutures. For rabbits, external sutures are a bit like a piece of lint on a sweater. Rabbits tend to fuss with them, licking and pulling, and may actually remove one or two. Years ago, my own rabbits nagged at their spay sutures. Buried, dissolvable sutures make

ensure its long life and domesticity. There are several good reasons for this surgery.

Sexual maturity (at 5 months for the smaller breeds of rabbits, and 8 months for the larger bunnies, like angoras) brings a hormonal rush to both the male and female rabbit. Like male cats, mature male bunnies will mark or spray their territory with urine. This includes spraying through the wire mesh sides of the cage and onto the corners, walls, and furniture in your house when he's allowed out of his cage. Whether sprayed around the cage or even in just one room of your house, the odor of male rabbit urine is pungent and pervasive (although it doesn't hold a candle to the scent of male cat urine). In addition to

Signs of Pain

Caring for your rabbit includes keeping it healthy and making certain it gets medical treatment if needed. How can you tell if your rabbit is in pain? Look for these signs:

✔ Heart rate increases
✔ Pupils dilate
✔ Behavioral changes
  • Guarding (protecting painful areas)
  • Vocalizing (especially when touched or moved)
  • Licking, biting, scratching, or shaking an area
  • Exhibiting restlessness such as continually getting up and down and pacing
  • Grinding teeth and subsequent loss of appetite
  • Refusing to move around (with joint or gut pain)
  • Failing to groom, and looking unkempt as a result
  • Assuming abnormal resting postures, when animal seems "humped up" or seems to be sleeping
  • Failing to show usual patterns of inquisitiveness

If any of these signs are present, contact your veterinarian immediately.

these annoyances a thing of the past.

Pain management. Neither my male nor my female rabbits exhibited any sign of pain after their surgeries, once I got them home. I did not realize at the time that prey animals generally do not show obvious signs of pain. At least several days of pain medication should be administered to a rabbit following any invasive procedure. Failure to adequately treat pain can lead to GI stasis and potentially hypersensitize the rabbit to future painful stimuli. For procedures like gastric surgery, postoperative pain management is recommended to help reduce the fear, pain, and stress.

Gastritis/internal parasites. Like every other animal in the world, rabbits have a certain number of internal parasites. The good news is that internal parasites are rare in domestic rabbits because domestic rabbits generally have limited exposure to other rabbits, and their feet never touch what may be contaminated ground.

You may not know what conditions were like for your rabbit before you got her, so you need to know what life forms may be sharing the internal rabbit.

Coccidia are a big part of the internal parasite picture. These are round, chubby-looking protozoans that can gain a foothold in a very

The first sign of snuffles may be a runny nose, but this is not a simple malady.

feet immersed in her water dish. I took her to my veterinarian, who took a smear of the fecal material, examined it under a microscope, and diagnosed Coccidia. The treatment was a flavored, liquid antibiotic. On the third day of treatment, the diarrhea had ended and she began to pick at her hay. In a week, she was her sweet "hoppy" self again, although we continued medicating her for the full 2 weeks.

Digestive problems

Gastrointestinal problems can be a death-knell for your rabbit. As one breeder of English Spots explained to me, "Rabbits don't have much resistance when something goes wrong in their gut. They just die. One day they're fine, the next day they're dead in their cage." You may have no warning that something is wrong with your rabbit; you may have warning. There's not much time to act.

Enteritus complex. Enteritus is a general term that means simply an inflammation of the intestinal tract. Your rabbit may have soft stools or diarrhea; he probably will exhibit a below-normal body temperature and will stop feeding. He may fail to respond to things he usually likes a lot.

The cause is usually a pathogenic bloom of a bacteria that gains a foothold because of a change in diet, the loss of or not enough "good" gut microflora, stress, and

young rabbit and kill it within a few days unless prompt action is taken. They can infest either the liver or the intestines.

My own experience with coccidia was with my second rabbit, Sassafras. Sassy came from a chain pet store. I found her in a waist-height open bin (irresistible for rabbit selection, I can assure you) with other young rabbits. She was a beautiful young mini-lop with a mild case of diarrhea when I bought her. I thought that maybe it was the stress of being in an open cage, with everyone in the store picking her up, but instead of going away, the diarrhea worsened. By the second day home, she stopped hopping about in her screened play area. She picked only sporadically at her food. She sat apathetically, moving once to sit with her front

a genetic predisposition to gut dysfunction. Young rabbits or newly weaned animals are the most often affected and have the highest mortality. These rabbits don't yet have the normal gastrointestinal flora and have a high gastric pH, which allows for the proliferation of bacteria.

Treatment needs to be assertive. Increase gut mobility by adding fiber in the form of hay. Remove the stress. Rehydrate the rabbit, and support the growth of normal microflora. When a pathogenic bacteria has been identified, an antibiotic may be prescribed.

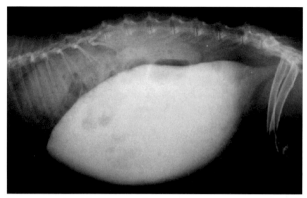

X-ray showing bladder sand.

Hairballs. Rabbits, being the furry creatures that they are, are also careful groomers, which can result in hairballs in their stomach. This is by no means uncommon, and usually the hairballs are passed as part of the digestive process. Rabbits cannot vomit, so the only way they can rid themselves of hairballs is to pass them. We used to think that ingested hair or a hairball was the reason why so many bunnies got ill and quickly died. Now we realize that gastrointestinal stasis is far more likely to kill your rabbit than a hairball.

The first treatment is rehydration, via IV's for your rabbit and rehydration of the stomach contents. A high-fiber supplement may be used to increase gut motility; Oxbow has a Critical Care Formula that is administered orally by means of a syringe.

Obviously prevention is far easier than the cure, and it comes down to diet. A high-fiber diet, meaning hay, is a real help in keeping gastric motility at its highest. If you feed a commercial pellet, check the label for fiber content, and look for one that offers a fiber content of 15% or more. The traditional rabbit diet of unlimited amounts of loose hay combined with limited amounts of high-fiber rabbit pellets is a very good way to help prevent any gastric upsets.

Grooming, on your part, not just the rabbit's, is another way to prevent or reduce the incidence of hairballs.

Ingested hair after it passes through the digestive system.

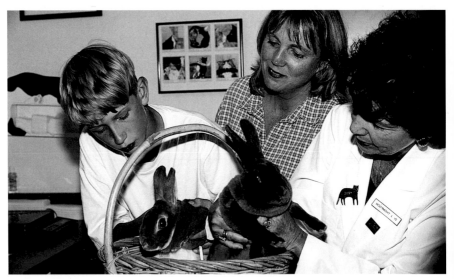

A pair of Rex rabbits are in for their annual wellness checkup.

Bladder stones. If your rabbit shows sign of straining and debilitating pain and yet seems unable to pass her urine, bladder stones may be the problem. Rabbits that have a diet high in calcium have to excrete that excess calcium as calcium carbonate. This is excreted through the kidneys, as part of the urine. Sometimes the calcium carbonate accumulates as sludge in the bottom of the urinary bladder; generally it can be expressed through fluid diuresis and manual expression. It may be too thick to express or it may actually form a stone, which is when surgery is required. After the bladder is open, the stone or sludge is removed, and the bladder is irrigated to remove all traces of calcium carbonate. After the rabbit is again eating and released to you, you'll need to place her on a diet low in calcium.

Glossary

Agility A type of rabbit training that promotes a rabbit's natural ability to quickly maneuver a series of jumps, tunnels, and climbing obstacles. In competitive agility, rabbits and their owners race against the clock.

Agouti color pattern A hair shaft with three or more bands of color. It is usually dark at the base with two or more alternating light/dark areas toward the tip of the hair shaft. This pattern is typical of the Chinchilla rabbit and Belgian hare.

Bell ears Lop ears with large tips.

Belt Area just behind the shoulders where the colored portion meets the white portion.

Blaze White line on the face running from the nose to the eyes.

Blemishes In a show rabbit, flaws or defects that affect the appearance of the rabbit.

Breed A race or special class of domestic rabbits that have specific size, body and ear shape, fur markings, and texture. Breeds are further subdivided into varieties, like the blue, black, and tortoise varieties of the Dutch breed.

Breeding certificate Written certificate by the owner of a stud buck, showing its pedigree and the date of breeding to a particular doe. Proves the ancestry of the young.

Broken tail A disqualification in show rabbits.

Buck An unaltered male rabbit.

Butterfly Dark-colored area surrounding the rabbit's nose. Typically seen in checkered giant and English spot breeds.

Clicker, clicker training Using a hand-held clicker, the same that is used in dog training, as positive reinforcement in rabbit training.

Competition course The pathway a competing rabbit is to follow, moving over or through the jumps and obstacles. The course is set up inside a course area.

Corrections The actions a handler takes to position/lift the rabbit into place for a second try at a jump.

Dam Mother rabbit.

Disqualification The end result of a major transgression on the part of a handler. The handler and the rabbits under that handler's aegis may no longer compete in the event, and any results are declared null and void. If the transgression is serious enough, prior records can be struck.

A fuzzy lop clears a backyard high jump.

Doe An unaltered female rabbit.

Enrichment Offering a changing living environment to a changed or house rabbit.

Faults In agility or jumping, knocking a bar down or landing in the middle of a broad jump or a water course; also going around an jump or obstacle. In rabbit shows, also imperfections in color that affect rank but do not disqualify the rabbit. In Rex rabbits, light toenails are a fault.

Final The best jumpers/agility rabbits (those with no faults) compete against each other.

Foreign color Any imperfection of color different from the standard for the breed.

Gestation The length of pregnancy in a doe. It's short, just 28 to 32 days, and the female can breed again in just 30 days.

Grooming Brushing, caressing, or combing the rabbit; it serves as an act of bonding between rabbits or between rabbit and owner.

Guard hair Longer coarser hair that protects the softer undercoat. Gives luster to the coat.

Hair ball The accumulation of shed fur in the belly of a rabbit. Unless passed or removed, this results in the death of the rabbit.

Intermediate In competition, a rabbit older than 6 months and younger than 8 months.

Junior In competition, a rabbit younger than 6 months old.

Kindle or kindling The rabbit-centered term for giving birth, as in "my doe kindled four young kits."

Kits Baby rabbits that weigh less than 16 ounces.

Lapin French for rabbit. In the rabbit trade, it means dyed rabbit fur.

Malocclusion Upper and lower teeth do not meet evenly resulting in uneven wear of the teeth.

Molt Shedding the fur. Molting usually occurs in spring and in fall.

Palpate To examine a female rabbit by feel to determine pregnancy. Unless you're showing rabbits, you have no need to do this; get your rabbit spayed.

Pelage The fur coat.

Presiding judge The judge presiding over the event currently in progress, or over the event in question.

Self-colored Having the same color all over the body, with no ticking or shading.

Snuffles Vernacular terms for a very contagious infection of nasal passages and lungs. It is very difficult to cure completely if not caught early.

Spraddled legs Forefeet bowed out when viewed from the front; hind feet are turned out from the hock joint. Usually found in rabbits kept on smooth surfaces when young and usually permanent.

Stress Placing a rabbit in an unfamiliar situation without a place of refuge or escape.

Tattoo The permanent identification marking placed in a rabbit's ear by professional breeders. The ARBA number goes in the right ear, breeder's numbers go in the left ear.

Ticking Wavy distribution of guard hair that is different in color from the undercoat. The ticking may be black ticking, such as in Chinchilla and Belgian hares.

Warren The tunnel complex occupied by wild rabbits or the walled enclosures used to contain captive rabbit colonies.

Wool The pulled or shed guard hair fur of an angora, usually 2½ to 4 inches (5 to 10 cm) long and fine in texture.

Useful Addresses and Literature

America Rabbit Breeders Association
P.O. Box 5667
Bloomington, Illinois 61702
Phone: 309-664-7500
Fax: 309-664-0941
info@arba.net
    The ARBA serves to promote the domestic rabbit and cavy fancy as well as all facets of the industry, including commercial and scientific research facilities.

Hopping and Agility Groups

The Danish Hopping Club
http://www.kaninhop.dk/uk/

Rabbit Hopping Organization of America
Linda Hoover
http://pets.groups.yahoo.com/group/RabbitHoppingUSA-Agility/
Rabbit hopping information and resources

The American Association of Sporting Events for Rabbits
Lyne Peterson
http://sports.groups.yahoo.com/group/AASERabbits/
Creating standards for all rabbit sports in the United States

Iowa Hopping Group
http://sites.google.com/site/iowa-hopping/

Breed Specialty Groups

There is at least one specialty group for all rabbit breeds. Groups for breeds mentioned in this book are included here.

American Belgian Hare Club
Jess Barabe
86 River Street
Riverside, RI 02915
401-433-2820
lapinrouge99@yahoo.com

American Fuzzy Lop Rabbit Club
Deb Levisay
1007 Country Club Lane
Spencer, IA 51301
712-262-4139
hbbuneez@yahoo.com

American Dutch Rabbit Club
Rick Billups
488 Pratt Road
Blanchester, OH 45107
937-655-8657
AmDutchClub@aol.com

American Federation of New
Zealand Rabbit Breeders
John T Neff
1351 Holder Lane
Geneva, FL 32732
407-349-0450
newzealand1121@aol.com

American Mini Lop Rabbit Club
Wendy Brabender
2829 Evergreen Drive
Cambridge, WI 53523
608-423-3164
frogpond@bminet.co

American Netherland Dwarf
Rabbit Club
Susan Clarke Smith
864 Barkers Creek Road
Whittier, NC 28789
828-586-9698
andrcsecy@yahoo.com

American Thrianta Rabbit Breeders
Association
Tina Reif
205 Mountain Laurel Lane
West Union, SC 29696
864-718-1118
creif1@yahoo.com

Champagne D'Argent Rabbit Federation
Lenore Gergen
14914 Bittersweet Court
Rosemount, MN 55068
651-283-0202
cdrfsec@aol.com

Havana Rabbit Breeders Association
Tanya Zimmerman
N9487 Walnut Road
Clintonville, WI 54929
715-823-5020
havanasecretary@yahoo.com

Lop Rabbit Club of America
Sandy Bennett
323 Macedon Drive
Lexington, SC 29073
lrcasec@gmail.com

National Angora RBC, Inc.
Margaret Bartold
909 Highway E
Silex, MO 63377
573-384-5866
tomar5866@windstream.net

National Federation of Flemish Giant Rabbit Breeders, Inc.
Karen Clouse
7587 West Cromwell Road
Ligonier, Indiana 46767
260-220-9196
clousesflemish@ligtel.com

National Jersey Wooly Rabbit Club
Laurie Owen
660 W Riddle Avenue
Ravenna, OH 44266
330-620-1502
lowen@neo.rr.com

Index